LIFE AND TEACHING OF THE MASTERS OF THE FAR EAST

By Baird T. Spalding

Volume III

DeVorss & Co., *Publishers*
P.O. Box 550
Marina del Rey, CA 90294

Volume 3   ISBN: 0-87516-086-7
5-Volume Set   ISBN: 0-87516-538-9

Printed in the United States of America

THE LIFE AND TEACHING
OF THE
MASTERS OF THE FAR EAST

by Baird T. Spalding

Baird T. Spalding, whose name became legend in metaphysical and truth circles during the first half of the 20th century, played an important part in introducing to the Western world the knowledge that there are Masters, or Elder Brothers, who are assisting and guiding the destiny of mankind. The countless numbers of letters that have come in through the years, from all over the world, bear testimony of the tremendous help received from the message in these books.

Partial listing of the contents of the five volumes:

Volume I: Introduction of the Master Emil—Visit to the "Temple of Silence"—Astral projection—Walking on Water—Visit to the Healing Temple—Emil talks about America—The Snowmen of the Himalayas—New Light on the teachings of Jesus.

Volume II: Visit to the Temple of the Great Tau Cross—Visit with the Master Jesus—Jesus discusses the nature of hell; the nature of God—The Mystery of thought vibrations—Jesus feeds the multitude—An account of a healing experience—Jesus and Buddha visit the group.

Volume III: One of the masters speaks of the Christ consciousness—The nature of cosmic energy—The creation of the planets and the worlds—The trip to Lhasa—Visit at the Temple Pora-tat-sanga—Explaining the mystery of levitation—A doubter becomes convinced of the existence of Jesus.

Volume IV: This material was first presented as "The India Tour Lessons." Each chapter has text for study, as well as guides to teachers for developing and interpreting the material. Among subjects covered: The White Brotherhood—The One Mind—Basis of coming social reorganization—Prana.

Volume V: Material taken from lectures given by Mr. Spalding in California during the last two years of his life. There is also a brief biographical sketch. Partial contents: Camera of past events—Is there a God—The divine pattern—The reality—Mastery over death—The law of supply.

Each of the 5 volumes has approximately 175 pages.

PUBLISHER'S NOTE

Both Mr. Spalding and Mr. DeVorss (who knew Mr. Spalding personally) died in the 1950's. The people who were associated with Mr. Spalding on the tour have also passed on. We are therefore without contact with anyone who has firsthand knowledge of the work, and the books themselves are now the only source of information. To our knowledge, there is no map available of the tour, and we know of no photographs. We have tried at various times to locate additional records, as well as camera information, but without success. We sincerely regret that we have no additional information to offer.

DEVORSS & COMPANY

FOREWORD

DEAR READER, you are not only a reader but a friend whom I have met face to face and conversed with, just as you have met and conversed with each of the characters in this book. I am certain they know you and look upon you as a close friend. They surround you with the full glory of the Divine Light of Life, Love, and Wisdom; and by surrounding you thus, they aid you in your understanding.

They enfold you in the ever-present Divine Light of Life, Love, and Wisdom which is theirs to send out and to give. They see you always enfolded in this Omnipresent Divine Presence. They see you seated on your own throne as a true king or queen, ruling through and by this Divine Presence. They envisage you knowing and accomplishing your Divine Mission, always alive, always peaceful and happy, always the Divine You. They see not only you but the whole human family, divine and pure, and every created thing or form as divine, created in the image and likeness of the divine; not one nor one sect nor one creed but all and that all inclusive.

None can appreciate these great people save those who have been admitted to the quiet of their sacred places and thoughts. They LIVE Truth, which is a part of the Universe itself. Life is really traceable back into the misty past which bears to us the accomplishments of hundreds of thousands of past centuries. To us, life is bound about by every limitation and convention. To them, life is boundless, ceaseless, unending bliss and happiness; the longer the span of life, the greater the joy and the more worthwhile the living.

None that understand and love these people can doubt their teachings; neither can he doubt their true sincerity when he has partaken of their hospitality.

The western world looks to the outer, thereby touching the hem of the garment. The eastern puts on the robe but not as a garment that may be laid aside.

The West polish the vessel of the lamp. The East fan the flame that it may give forth a more intense light.

The West look to the outer with longing eyes, back of which is the glow of spiritual vision, the seeking of true knowledge. The East know that flesh must be illumined by the light of the flame that is first kindled from within, then allowed to shine forth to the without as the full blaze of the noonday sun.

The West name themselves material. The East live truly in the allness of spirit. They behold each and every one living by compelling, impelling, sustaining Spirit, — it matters not what the location, be it in the great snows of Alti Himalaya, the busy modern city, or the most secluded monastery.

That which to the western world seems miraculous and unbelievable is to the poised Hindu thought, the natural outcome of the acceptance and the bringing forth of Spirit, that which is set forth as God in manifest form. They that are fully alive know full well that there is far more than that which comes under their personal recognizance; in fact, there is much more than ever has been dreamed of in any philosophy.

Therefore, there are no apologies offered for this book or for those which have preceded it.

When you look longingly with a clear vision toward an accomplishment, it is your divine heritage to command that you place yourself in such a receptive attitude that the ability is already yours to bring forth your ideal.

God speaks through the God-man today just as God has spoken down the long ages. The knowledge which the people in this book convey is by no means new, although the presentation brings a new light to the western world.

The main object of their lives is to give knowledge and enlightenment to humanity through pure knowledge, aflame with love. Their great mission is to pave the way toward peace and harmony through man's great power to accomplish. They are the greatest friends of true science, religion, and philosophy; and they proclaim these as well as all men, brothers, as Truth is one. Thus science becomes the golden thread upon which the pearls are strung.

The day is here in which a large portion of humanity has already outgrown the old concept of Divinity. They have lost their faith in teachings based upon faith alone; they have learned that to be good in order to gain a heavenly reward after death is a fallacy, a very low ideal, — this idea of being good for the reward's sake and the special privilege of playing harps and singing psalms forever. They have realized that this is an expression of self-interest only and completely foreign to the teachings of the Christ of God, the God-man fully alive.

The idea of death is foreign to — in fact, it is a direct contradiction of — the divine purpose and is not in accord with the law of the Cosmos or its vibrant radiations. Neither is it in accord with the teachings of Jesus.

The church and the graveyard are often in the

same field. This alone is a direct acknowledgment that Christian teachings have not been even comprehended. The Christ-man has spoken and the listening ear has heard, "If a man believes in me, he shall never die." The God-man knows that the one who is in sin or lives with sinful vibrations surrounding him dies, and unto him "the wages of sin is death"; but the gift of God to the God-man, is eternal life—God made manifest to God-man in the kingdom of God here on earth, the human body perfect in the flesh, when man lives true to the God vibration and wholly in that vibratory thought.

The people in this book have taken God out of the realm of the supernatural and of superstition and have placed Him wholly in vibratory frequency, knowing that as they keep their bodies in the divine vibration, they never grow old and never die.

When the vibrations of their bodies are lowered or allowed to slow down, death ensues. In fact, these people know that when the mistake of death is accomplished, the body is vibrating at such a low rate that the emanating life-vibrations are actually crowded out of the body temple and that those vibrating life-emanations still hold together and maintain the same form which the body had when they were crowded out. Those emanations have intelligence and still revolve around a central nucleus or sun which attracts and holds them together. These emanating particles are surrounded by an intelligent emanation that assists them to keep their form and from which they again draw substance to erect another temple. This is in direct accord and works in complete harmony with the intelligence that has been built around the body during their life cycle. If that intelligence vibrates at a low frequency or, in other words, is weak, it loses contact with the emanations of life and energy that have been forced out of the body (or form of clay after the life-emanations have left it) and the emanations finally disperse and return to the source, then complete death is accomplished; but, if the intelligence is strong, vibrant, and active, it takes full charge immediately and a new body is instantly assembled. A resurrection has taken place; and through that resurrection man is perfected in the flesh. Not all can hear or accept such a revelation. "He that hath ears to hear, let him hear." [Mark 4:9.] He whose understanding is developed sufficiently, is able to comprehend.

Thus, large portions of humanity are developing a science through which they are again discovering that God has always lived in man and with humanity; yet they for a time have not known God, they have only lost sight of the God-man.

To those of whom I have written I dedicate this book, as well as the books that have been published. At the feet of these near and dear ones I lay my deepest respect and gratitude and in no way do I feel that I am conferring upon them the honor due them.

We went doubting; we left with the greatest regrets, loving them every one, feeling that we had gained a truer and deeper insight into the science of Life and True Living.

(Signed) BAIRD T. SPALDING

CHAPTER I

AFTER those assembled had departed, my associates and I stayed on, loath to leave the place
where we had witnessed such a transformation.
No words can describe our feelings and the tremendous uplift of those last hours.

The words, "ALL FOR ONE, ONE FOR ALL,"
blazed forth as vividly as when they first appeared.
We did not talk, we could not say a word. Although
we were in the same general position until daylight,
we had no sense of being confined in a room. Our
bodies seemed to emit a brilliant light and, wherever we walked we had no sense of limiting walls,
although just previous to the experience we were in a
room hewed from solid rock. There did not seem to
be a floor under our feet; yet we moved freely in any
direction.

Words absolutely fail to describe our thoughts and
sensations. We even walked beyond the confines of
the room and the cliff; yet we had no feeling of being
hampered. Our garments and everything about us
seemed to radiate a pure white light. Even after
sunrise this light seemed brighter than that of the
sun. We seemed to be in a great sphere of light and
we could look through this crystal ray and see the sun
as it appeared far away, shrouded in a haze. It
actually seemed cold and uninviting compared with
the place where we stood. Although the thermome-
ter registered 45 degrees below zero and the country
was covered with snow that sparkled in the morning
sunlight, in the place where we were there was a

consciousness of warmth, peace, and beauty that surpasses expression. It was one occasion in which thoughts could not be put into words.

Here we stayed for three more days and nights with no thought of rest or refreshment. There was not a sign of fatigue or weariness and, as we looked back upon the time, it seemed as if it passed in an instant. Yet we were conscious of each other's presence and of the passing of the hours.

There was no sunrise or sunset, just a continuous glorious day; not a vague dream but every moment an actual reality. And what a vista of the future opened before us! The horizon seemed to be pushed back into eternity; or, as our Chief expressed it, it seemed to be expanding into a boundless and eternal sea of throbbing, pulsating life. And the great beauty of it all was that it was for all to see and know — not for just a few, but for all.

On the fourth day, our Chief suggested that we go below to the room of the records in order to again take up our work of translation. Upon making the move to proceed, we found ourselves standing all together in the room.

I can but let the reader picture our astonishment and joy. We had moved two stories down and accomplished two flights of stairs without the least physical exertion on our part and without the least knowledge of the accomplishment. Yet there we were in the room among the records where we had been working. It was all aglow with light, the place was warm and cheerful, and we could move anywhere we wished without the least effort.

When we took up one of the tablets and placed it in a convenient place for study, its context and meaning were translated to us perfectly. When we began writing these translated conclusions, suddenly a whole page of manuscript would be filled with the text in our own handwriting. All we need do, was to place the pages together in manuscript form.

In this way we finished manuscript after manuscript of these translations. By two o'clock that afternoon we had finished and filed twelve manuscripts of over four hundred pages each and we experienced not the least fatigue from this pleasant occupation.

We were so engrossed that we were unconscious of the presence of others in the room until our Chief stepped forward with a greeting. We all looked up to see Jesus, Emil, our hostess, and Chander Sen, — the man of the records, whom we had at first called the old man of the records but whom we now knew as "the young man." There were also Bagget Irand and a stranger to whom we were introduced as Ram Chan Rah. We later learned his familiar name to be Bud Rah.

A table was cleared and prepared for a meal. We sat down and after a few moments of silence, Jesus spoke:

"Almighty and All-Pervading Father Principle, which shines forth ever triumphant from within us out to all the world and is the light, love, and beauty which we are experiencing this day and which we always experience if we only will, we bow before this altar on which burns the undying fire of perfect love, harmony, true wisdom, unending devotion, and pure humility. This sacred light shines steadily on, undimmed, from within the souls of those who are now gathered at this, the altar of true fatherhood, sonship, and devoted brotherhood. This divine light does shine forth from these near and dear ones, out and out to the most remote places of all the world, that all may see its great light and may experience its undimmed and unquenchable love. The rays of this all-pervading light, beauty, and purity shine through the receptive souls and hearts of those who are gathered at this, your altar. We are now conscious of these all-consuming and embracing rays of love and we send them forth and they transmute, blend, and harmonize all mankind.

"It is the true and the pure Christ of God, standing forth from each and all, that we salute and stand face to face with, equal to — one with God.

"Again we salute God, our Father, right within and standing forth."

After Jesus ceased speaking, we all arose upon the suggestion that we return to the room where our former experience had taken place. As we started toward the door, we realized that we are already there.

This time we were conscious of moving but not conscious of the cause of locomotion. As soon as we expressed the desire, we were actually in the upper room. Although the shadows of evening were well advanced, our way was perfectly lighted and we found all aglow with the rich beauty and effulgence that had been there when we departed.

The reader will recall it was in the room we had just left that Chander Sen returned to us after being brought back from what we looked upon as death.

To us that room was a shrine and it seemed aglow with all possibilities, a sanctified place where we ourselves had been able to step forth to a greater accomplishment than, as mortals, we had previously known.

From that time on till April 15th, the day of our departure, not a day or night passed that we did not all meet together for at least one hour. During this time the room never again assumed the appearance of solid rock. It seemed as though we could always see through those walls into infinite space. It was in that room that the bonds limiting consciousness were removed. It was there that a great vista of the future opened to us. We all sat down at the table and Jesus resumed the conversation.

"It takes a true motivating thought, focused on a central absorbing point or ideal to bring forth or accomplish and you, as well as all mankind, can become that motivating center. Not one thing comes forth unless man first expresses the ideal.

"At one time man was fully conscious that he was this motivating center and lived fully conscious of his inheritance and dominion. He lived consciously in a condition that you term heaven. All but a few have let go of this divine gift and today the great majority are absolutely unconscious of this divine quality which is mankind's true inheritance.

"What man has done once, he can accomplish again. This is the principle back of the endless array of life and manifestation that you see all around you and includes your own life, together with that of every existing thing, as every existing thing has life. Ere long science will give you ample grounds for saying that things are not material, as science will soon see that all things can be reduced to one primal element containing innumerable particles universally distributed, responding to vibratory influences, and all in perfect and absolute equilibrium or balance.

"Hence, it follows on mathematical grounds alone that it took some definite movement, some initial action, to draw together the infinite particles of this all-pervading universal natural substance, in order to bring them into form as selective objects.

"This power did not originate wholly within a particle, but is a power greater, yet at one with the particle and you, through your thought and definite action, co-operating with the vibration, give selectivity to these particles. Thus will physical science be

16

compelled to understand through necessary deductions, so that scientists will recognize the presence of a power, which, at this time, is not understood because it is inactive; and which is inactive only because it is not recognized.

"But, when recognized and communed with by man and brought into actual expression, it is fully capable of separating certain specific areas for the specific display of this universal cosmic energy.

"Then there is built up what you look upon as a material universe, with all its different manifestations, by an orderly process of evolution. If orderly, then each stage must lay the foundation perfectly for the greater development of the stage that is to follow. If you can accomplish progress in perfect order and harmony of thought and action, you are in actual accord with power and this power brings forth, on an unlimited scale, the faculty of selecting the means to an end. You distribute life and energy under a recognized order of cosmic progression.

"This, then, is not a material universe as you have thought. That is only your definition of it. It came forth from spirit and it is spiritual, if you will define it as such. This is orderly, true, basic. If orderly, it is scientific; if scientific, it is intelligent, it is life united with intelligent life.

"Life coupled to and guided by intelligence, becomes volition and, through volition, it becomes vocation.

"Spirit is the primary, vibrating, originating power; and you may enter into spirit and use its power by the simple acceptance or knowing that it does exist; then let it come forth, and the whole of spirit is at your command. To you it becomes an ever-potent spring of perpetual and original life right within yourself.

"This does not take long years of study, nor need

you go through training or hardships or deprivation. Know and accept that this vibration does exist. Then let it flow through you.

"You are one with Great Creative Mind Substance; thus, you know that all things do exist. If you will but see that Divine Principle, Great Principle, Good Principle, God Principle is all there is, — that it fills all space, is all — then you are that principle; and, as you stand forth in your Christ Dominion and give out this principle, you, by your very thought, word, and act give this principle greater activity. Thus, one more has found his dominion and is using God power and sending it out. As you give out this power, it flows to you. As you give, more is pressed upon you to give and you will find you cannot deplete the supply.

"This does not mean going into a closet and hiding yourself. This is getting quiet right where you are, even in the busy so-called turmoil of life, under the most trying circumstances. Then life is not turmoil; it is quiet, contemplative, and compulsive.

"The outer activity is as nothing compared with the greater activity that you now realize and are one with. This is getting quiet right where you are, seeing God standing forth from you, — closer than breathing, nearer than hands and feet, — with your whole thought action centered on God.

"Who is God? Where is the God that your whole thought action is centered or focused upon?

"God is not a great being outside of you, that you are going to bring within and then present to the world. God is that power which is generated and exhilarated by your own thought action. It is true that this power is within and all about you, but it is inactive until you think of it and know that it does exist. Then you see it flowing forth from you in limitless measure. You present it to the world and the

18

world is benefited by your presentation. You, your-self, must present the accomplishment by putting forth the driving force of all Good, God your Father, the power to accomplish, behind every thought and act. Now you are God fulfilling or filling full the accomplishment. This is God, the true and only God, standing forth from you.

"You are then God the Father, the husbandman, the amplifier and the projector, the definite and positive accomplisher. It is then that legions fly to do your bidding.

"The moment you say wholeheartedly, with rev-erence and deep meaning, that God is in his Holy Temple and know that this temple is your pure body, just as you present it and as you truly stand today, that you, the true Christ, live one with God right within this temple, and that your exalted body is a holy abiding place, a whole and all-inclusive abode, you are an energizer, an all-including and outpouring vessel for this true and divine principle to flow through. Then you pour out more and more of the God which you are and which you love.

"You worship, you praise, and with your ever-expanding love, you pour out to all mankind that they may see the Christ, the God-man standing forth triumphant.

"Now you say with the keenest joy, 'Whosoever will, let him come and drink deeply of the waters of pure life.' Those who do this will never thirst again. This power you are using and sending forth is God. The Son accomplishes readily what the Father accomplishes. This is also being humble to and bow-ing before this great power. This is true humility stepping forth in humble mien, one with your own driving force and power.

"By constantly contemplating, praising, blessing and giving thanks to this power you increase its flow and, as you do this, it becomes potent and more readily accessible to you.

"Thus, I say, pray without ceasing. Your daily life is true prayer.

"By first KNOWING that this power does exist, then using it with absolute confidence, you soon become wholly conscious of it. You soon KNOW that it is all-inclusive in and through you. If you will but let it flow, it will rush to you in every instance: It flows to you as you let it flow from you. Stand forth as God and give it out. This is God your Father in you and you and your Father are one. Not servants but SONS, Sons of First Primal Cause. All that I AM has, is yours; for you are I AM.

"It is not I who do the work, it is I AM in the Father and the Father in me brings forth the great accomplishment. As you know that you work, one with the Father, there are no limitations, no boundaries; you know it is your divine right to accomplish all things.

"Then follow *me only as I follow* the Christ, the true Son, the only-begotten of the Father; and, as I bring forth and present God, I do bring forth God from within. Then will it be said all are God.

"The greatest sermon ever given is 'BEHOLD GOD.' This means seeing God standing forth in all glory right within and from you and from all others also. When you behold God and nothing else but God, you love and worship God and God alone; you truly behold God. You are the Lord, the Lawgiver, the dispenser of the Law.

"When you pray, enter your closet, the secret chamber of your own soul. There, pray to your Father within; and your Father, who hears, does reward you openly. Pray and give thanks that you are able to give forth more of God to the whole world.

"Does this not give you a higher and more lofty outlook, a broader perspective, a nobler ideal?"

Here the talk ended. We all arose from the table and our friends bade us goodnight and departed. We stayed on for a time and talked over the experiences, then decided to return to our lodgings in the village. As we arose, the thought immediately presented itself, "How are we to proceed without a light?" and all except the Chief voiced this thought.

Then he said, "You can see how definitely habit fixes itself upon us and how desperately we cling to old ideas. Here we are, completely immersed in light. It has not dimmed because of the absence of those we have grown to love so dearly. Is this not an occasion where we can step forth and show our own self-reliance, our own ability to be and to accomplish the things that we have experienced? Let us at least extend this to ourselves and have the courage to take the step toward the accomplishment.

"We are leaning so hard upon our wonderful friends that it actually hurts to have them leave us for a moment. I can see, as they already know, that if we do not become self-reliant in these small things, we will never accomplish the larger things; and I do not doubt for an instant that they have left in order to give us the opportunity of proving the accomplishment. Let us rise to the emergency and be above it."

As we started, one of the party suggested that we meditate on the method of procedure, but the Chief in a firm voice said, "No, if we go, we go now. After what we have seen and experienced, we must act and make these acts definite or we do not deserve any consideration." Whereupon we proceeded down the stairs, through the different rooms, through the tunnel, and down the ladder to the village.

As we walked along, our way was completely lighted; our bodies seemed without weight and we moved with the utmost ease. We arrived at our lodgings overjoyed by the accomplishment. From that time on until we left the village we traveled where we pleased without artificial light. Our lodgings lighted up as we entered the rooms and the warmth and beauty surpassed any power of description.

We retired almost immediately. Needless to say we did not awaken till late the next morning.

CHAPTER II

THE next morning we had our breakfast at the lodge, then went directly to the upper room of the Temple. There was no visible concept of the confines of a room, nor any evidence of limitation and so, we moved freely with no thought of exertion. When we were ready to go below to the room of the records, we were there. As we had accomplished this without the presence of our friends, we realized the reason for their withdrawal and were very much elated over our attainment.

The first of April was fast approaching. We had finished the records in the Temple rooms and had taken up the work of making measured drawings of the numerous characters and many carvings cut in the rocks outside. This work was going along very nicely because of our all-absorbing interest. One afternoon a messenger came to the village and, as the villagers gathered around him, we saw that something unusual was happening. We dropped our work and proceeded to the village. We met our hostess and were informed that the messenger had brought the information that a party of bandits was at large in the valley below.

This caused considerable uneasiness among the inhabitants, as this village had been the focal point of attempted raids for many years. The report had gone far and wide that the Tau Cross Temple was the hiding place for vast treasure. The many attempts to rob the village had failed. The bands had in a great measure attributed former failures to the resistance of the people who lived in the valley below. A number of the bands had now concentrated their combined forces and a band of about four thousand well-mounted and armed men were preying upon and devastating the valley, in order to discourage the resistance of the inhabitants in closer proximity to the little village of the Tau Cross. They hoped by this method that the raid would be more successful.

The messenger also appealed for protection for the remaining inhabitants, as a great many had already been destroyed and they had reached the limit of their resistance. He was told that there was no one in the village who could be sent but our hostess assured him that he could return to his home and that no harm would come to his people. We went on with our work, noting the uneasiness of the villagers; and that uneasiness was communicated to us.

The next morning we again resumed our work as we were very anxious to complete the references for our records. We were certain they would give a complete and accurate history and, also, references as to where other records could be found. Thus we could trace the history of this older and extremely enlightened civilization that occupied this vast and now most remote portion of the world.

We were disturbed by the possibility of losing this collection by reason of the bandit raids. As the results of our work, this collection was all assembled in the rooms of the records, where they had hitherto withstood a number of similar raids from the same source.

That evening we talked to our hostess about the possibility of the formulation of some plan to aid the villagers and voiced our surprise and wonder at the absence of our friends. We were told that, as an appeal for aid had been made by the messenger, the bandits would be obliged to stop their raids or they would destroy themselves.

We retired that evening fully assured that we had been over-solicitous of our own safety. We arose early and were preparing to resume work, when the same messenger appeared with the news that the raids had ceased upon the inhabitants and that the band had concentrated their entire force about twenty miles down the valley for an apparent concerted last drive on our little village.

As our hostess and little party stood talking to the messenger, who was surrounded by a group of the villagers, a horseman rode into the village and came toward us. In coming toward us, as he passed smaller groups of congregated people, he was apparently recognized. They immediately dispersed and fled in terror. As he neared our group, the messenger called out the horseman's name and then, the messenger as well as the others took refuge in flight, evidently fearing that the horseman was being followed by the band.

Our hostess and ourselves were the only ones left as we awaited the nearer approach of the horseman. He reined in his horse and with much gusto addressing our Chief, began to speak, saying that the bandits were fully aware we were strangers and that they were acquainted with our mission. He spoke in a tongue that none of us understood. He saw our bewilderment and asked if there were not some one that could interpret. Our hostess turned and faced the man as he sat upon his horse and asked if she could be of service. At first he looked as though he had received a severe electric shock. He, however, sufficiently recovered his composure to fairly spring from his horse. He rushed toward her with outstretched hand, exclaiming, "*You* here?" in the language that we understood. Then he placed his hands to his forehead and prostrated himself before her, begging her pardon. Our hostess directed him to arise and deliver his message. We could see her form stiffen and, for a moment, her features almost blazed with anger. So intense was her display of emotion that, for an instant, we, as well as the man himself, were absolutely startled out of our composure. The words "Coward, murderer, step forth and deliver your message" almost leapt from her lips. The man again went to his knees. Again the words blazed forth, "Stand up! Are you so debased that you dare not stand?"

We did not wonder at the man's abject terror, for we, as well as he, were absolutely rooted to the spot, unable to move.

I am certain had it been humanly possible for the man to have done so, he would have fled from the scene. For the moment he, as well as ourselves, had lost all power of speech and action, he crumpled to the ground, limp and apparently lifeless, his eyes staring and his mouth agape.

This was the first and only time in our experience with these people of superior powers that we had seen one of them give expression in any way to violent emotion. We were as terrified as the bandit. The vibrations hit us just as distinctly as the force of a tremendous explosion, accompanied by an electric shock that not only paralyzed speech but our muscles as well. That is the only way I can describe the sensation. Coming from that slight and unassuming fragile form, do you wonder that these vibrations paralyzed us into inaction?

Although this situation lasted only a moment, it seemed hours before the tension relaxed. We were as transfixed as statues; yet there flooded over us in that instant a great pity for the bandit and we found ourselves longing to go to his assistance. This was the reaction of all; yet we only stood and stared at our hostess.

Almost at once the condition changed. At first a startled look came over her face, then it changed to the same kindly expression that we were accustomed to, and there swept over us such a wave of compassion that we rushed to the prostrate form on the ground. Our hostess was bending over him, her hand clasping his. Again we were mystified and could only say, "Will wonders never cease?"

The man soon regained consciousness, was helped to his feet, and was made as comfortable as possible on a bench near by. He absolutely refused to enter any of the houses.

Our hostess then apologized for the vehemence which she had expressed, noting the effect it had upon us. Our flesh was quivering and it required some time for us to regain our composure.

She explained that this man was the leader of one of the most notorious bands that infested that portion of the Gobi. His name, if mentioned at all, was spoken with awe, as he was the most fearless and ruthless of characters. His familiar title literally translated meant "Consummate Black Devil released from Hell." His features portrayed "en masque" were kept in many villages and worn by those participating in the ritual of driving the evil spirit from the village and its inhabitants.

Our hostess had contacted this man on two former occasions when attempted raids had failed and each time he had evidenced the deepest hatred for her and our friends in general, going out of his way to harass them and sending violent messages from time to time, which they ignored completely. His sudden appearance alone had brought the past indignities so forcibly before her that she, for the time being, had lost control of her emotions.

Having fully regained her composure, she walked over to the man. At her approach, he made a futile attempt to arise, but was only able to draw himself together and sit more erect, the picture of abject fear. Hatred was delineated in every movement of his body, which was trembling as though stricken with palsy. Our hostess, now cool and collected, with no trace of fear or emotion, her face, features, and body as wonderfully cut as the most delicate cameo, presented an amazing contrast.

We wanted to remove the man at once and, although this thought was not expressed, our hostess raised her hand commanding silence. Our Chief realized that she was in charge of the situation and that anything we would attempt to do would only place us in a ludicrous position. We withdrew out of hearing while our hostess talked in low and quiet tones for quite some time before the man answered a word.

As he spoke, the lady motioned us to approach. We sat on the ground before them, glad to make any move that would relieve the tension of suspense. The bandit explained that he had prevailed upon his superior leaders to allow him to come as a peace emissary to treat with the people for the surrender of the supposed treasure that was concealed in the Tau Cross Temple. If the inhabitants would surrender the treasure, the bandits would agree not to molest them further, would agree to release all their prisoners (of which they claimed there were over three thousand), and would immediately leave the country and never again molest the inhabitants of the valley.

Our hostess told him there was no treasure that would be of any value to them. A thorough explanation of the fact was gone into, with an offer to conduct him through all the rooms of the Temple or any place he wished to go. He flatly refused this proposition, saying that he feared they would hold him as hostage, and no assurance upon our part could break down this fear.

Our hostess reassured him of our sincerity and he suddenly became convinced that we were honest in our statements. Then a situation difficult and alarming for him arose. He told us that he was the instigator of this plot and had fired the imaginations of the other bandits with the zeal for possessing the treasure and that he had painted a lurid picture of the fabulous wealth that would be theirs should he succeed. In fact he and his father had held their band together with promises of the possession of this treasure. He was the chief of the band that had consolidated with five other bands to carry out this raid.

The crux of this situation was that if he should return to his band with the information that there was no treasure, he would immediately be branded as a traitor and, as such, would be dealt with accordingly. He could not deter the band from the contemplated attack, as they would not believe him on account of his zeal in pressing the situation up to this point.

It was decidedly an embarrassing position for him. To our great surprise, our hostess offered to accompany him to the camp. Our protests were quietly overruled and she prepared to leave immediately. She assured us that she was in no danger but that if we went along, our presence would instill suspicion in the minds of the bandits, so that all would incur great danger. We meekly submitted. There was nothing else we could do.

The man mounted his horse and we assisted her to mount to the seat that was prepared behind him. As they rode from the village, they presented a never-to-be-forgotten picture, one that will live in our memories for all eternity—the bandit with doubt written all over his features and our hostess smiling back at us with the warm assurance that she would return by nightfall. We lost all interest in our work for the rest of the day and wandered aimlessly about the village until sunset.

We returned to the lodge to await the return of our hostess and, upon entering, we found the table loaded with good things to eat. You can imagine our astonishment to see her seated at the head of the table and greeting us with that radiant smile of hers. We were speechless; words failed us entirely. She assumed an air of mock hauteur and tried to say sternly, "Gentlemen, a greeting is in order"; whereupon we bowed and extended our salutations.

Then she continued, "I failed utterly to convince them but they did agree to give me an answer within the next three days. I know that the answer will be an attempted attack but I did save the life that poor creature for the time being, at least. We shall be obliged to prepare ourselves to withstand the siege; nothing will deter them from making the attempt."

I think that nearly all of us saw our fondest dreams and the results "go-a-glimmering" as the familiar saying has it. Our hostess read our inmost thoughts and repeated this poem:

When you come to the Red-Sea-place in your life,
    When, in spite of all you can do,
There is no way 'round, there is no way back,
    There is no other way but THROUGH:
Then know God with a soul serene,
    And the dark and the storm are gone.
God stills the wind. God stills the waves.
    God says to your soul, "GO ON!
GO ON! GO ON! GO ON!"

CHAPTER III

AFTER the meal was finished, we arose from the table, our hostess leading us into the garden. To our great surprise we found Jesus, Emil, Jast, and Bud Rah, seated. We joined the group and sat down. We could sense the inaudible sigh of relief and realized how much we had grown to rely upon these people. It was as though we had fastened ourselves to them with bands of steel. Somehow I saw that this we must not do. It was necessary for us to play our definite part in this great scheme of life, in order that we might not become mere puppets; we must stand wholly upon our own feet and rely wholly upon ourselves, or they would be obliged to sever the bands entirely. Our Chief talked freely upon this subject later.

The evening was still young and the soft glow of the fading sunset colors suffused everything with a luxuriance and beauty that one must see to appreciate. There was not a breath of air stirring, not even a sound to disturb the tranquility that seemed to engulf us. The bandit situation that we believed had weighed so heavily upon us but a moment before, had disappeared entirely.

It was calm and peaceful. There was that beautiful feeling of complete relaxation which again must be experienced to be understood. It was as though we were in a great stream of slowly moving light; we became suddenly aware that we heard the voice of Jesus but not in words. My only explanation is, that it was a pure rhythmic, flowing, vibratory influence that came to us in thought instead of words. The effect was much more pronounced than that of words; the rhythm and cadence were beyond description. Thoughts seemed to flood in and lodge; this was an entirely new experience.

As these thoughts or ideas came, we translated them into stenographic characters, then transposed them into words and sentences, later submitting them to these people for approval.

"When I say, 'Behold a Christ of God is here,' I behold the God-man standing forth. I see this body as the true temple of God, the perfect instrument or channel through which the Great Creative Principle flows and comes forth freely; then this creation is unadulterated in image, form, and likeness. I AM GOD. In this attitude I stand forth the master of every situation, the Christ of God triumphant.

"It is this ideal that I worship and that which I worship, I bring forth. I can in no way bring forth God if I AM does not present God to all humanity. In this attitude man stands forth the master of every situation; the Christ is triumphant, conquering. God and man are walking hand in hand, ONE. There is but one Principle, one Man."

One of our party thought for a moment and then asked, "How can we bring forth this light and make practical use of it?"

The answer came. "Let your body become a generator through which this Great Creative Radiating Principle flows. See this Principle as the emanation of all power; know that it is the principle of all power; then, like an electric generator, your body will collect and magnify this energy until you send it out as a stream of pure white light that nothing can resist and anything directed toward you cannot harm you.

"You can also send such intense impulses of electrical energy over these light beams that the body of the one attempting to harm you will be destroyed.

Any resistance to this energy immediately magnifies its volume and therefore its velocity. The ones setting up resistance against it or attempting to set up their personal will only harm themselves. If they do not set up any resistance to this light, it will pour its healing balm through them as well as it does through you.

"It is the pure God-beam and power, which blends with that of another at all times if there is no resistance to its free flow. It vibrates with the highest vibration. Consequently, all are vibrating in perfect harmony and accord and no harm can possibly come to them, as they are in unison with the God vibration. There is absolutely nothing that can harm another unless that one resists the God vibration. Vibration is life. Do you not see how you stand one with God at all times? In this attitude would there be a possibility of separation? The only separation is the resistance that causes the inharmony.

"Nothing can come near you when you stand in the Holy Mount, One with God. This is not a special privilege for a few, this is for all; I AM, the great absolute cause or source in which every child stands one with God. Thus all live under THE LAW, the highest vibratory thought action. There is not an inharmonious vibration that can enter this sphere, this throne, where all belong and are at home. This is your Divine Kingdom.

"You can also use this power to return false and harmful thoughts or desires that are directed toward you. You can, if you so desire, step up this white God-light-beam, endow it with God power, magnify and transform the energy the sender has given the thing or condition that was intended for you, then place it into your reflector and send it back to the sender with the velocity of light. When you return it in this way it is a beam of pure white light, instead of merely lowered vibrations, as it was sent out to you.

"When it reaches the sender, the impulses are so potent that it can destroy the body of the one who first put in motion the lower vibration. It matters not whether you know the sender or the location from which it came, the vibration will return to its source unerringly. The judgment or day of retribution has arrived. 'As you give, so you receive good measure (God measure) pressed down and running over.'

"You can transform God-power and send it out with such force that it is irresistible. These are the beams or rays of light that you see emanating from my body. These rays are emanating from your body, although they are not yet as potent; but as you go on and use this power, allied with Law and Principle, you will add potency to the light and can consciously direct it to accomplish any good desire.

"When the artist portrayed me at Gethsemane, the rays of light went out from my body instead of coming out from heaven to me. The light is the God-power generated from within my body, then sent out by the reflector. These beams go out from every body when that person stands forth as God in his divine heritage—the Christ of God ALL ONE.

"This is and can be made the definite motto of all humanity. Can there be discord between brothers if they become this all-absorbing One?

"Now, step up this white beam which is the God-beam upon which you send out God-power; endow it with God-power transformed, ten thousand or ten million times greater than that which has been sent out to you and which you are returning (this is as you decree); then let it flow back upon the same path that the vibrations of the thing traveled to you. When the person receives this ray and accepts it as coming from God, the attempted harm is all erased, forgiven, forgotten, and no harm can come to you or the sender of that harmful thought. You are both eye to eye one with God. Instead of inharmony, there is perfect harmony, you are again ONE.

"If the sender of the harmful thought does not accept the white ray which you have sent out in all its potency, his body will be destroyed. This pure white ray will completely erase every vibration of harm or discord if allowed to complete its perfect work. If resisted, there is nothing but a perfect erasure for the one who holds determinedly to the resistance. His resistance draws to him the whole creative principle, ADVERSELY, as to the square of the resistance set up. The square means multiplying the resistance four times.

"Thus you see that, as you send out good or evil, it will return to you fourfold.

"You are standing forth as the Lord or Law giving forth Good or God for evil but, even in this attitude, be truly humble, JUDGE NOT. Place every bit of love you possess upon this pure white ray and see well to it that it is the pure love of God that you are generating and sending forth. As you accomplish this, legions are at your command. You are still meek and humble, willing to follow on with the light. It is the pure light of God that you follow; and that light is life, love, purity and beauty, eternal and profound.

"There are seven centers in your body that can be used as reflectors. You can cause these central points to glow with a radiance far greater than any artificial light and, when you wish to send out this light, it glows with a greater potency and will reach farther than any electrical beam that can be projected.

"By setting all these centers aglow at the same time, you are completely surrounded by an armor that nothing can penetrate.

"You can send out the pure white ray of God, so energized that your body actually glows with a brilliancy far greater than that of the noonday sun. You stand forth Lord of Creation, the Lord of Hosts. You stand forth true and triumphant yet peaceful, loving, God enthroned in your body, and that body beautiful, spiritual, and divine."

As these vibrations came to us, the light emanating from the bodies of Jesus and his group was most difficult to behold; yet there was that vibrant brilliancy shining through, which resembled liquid gold. To our vision there seemed to be an indefiniteness, while to all of the other senses there was the solidity of rock. Again the vibrations came:

"In this way you can make your body completely invisible to mortal sight by focusing your entire thought fully and definitely upon the pure white God ray and letting it go forth from the seven centers as reflectors, in unison.

"Then, again you can step right out on either of these rays and present any picture that you wish to those that would do you harm. You can follow on this beam with the exact speed of light, and go where you will, instantly. Your body is invisible to those who do not see through and beyond the mortal. They are aware that there is something they do not understand; thus, they are susceptible to any picture you wish to present to them. That which they do not understand is mysterious or super-natural and the faculty which is developed through suspicion or superstition is easily misled. Thus you send out love to those that would do you harm and the energy they release reflects back to them.

"The picture of harm they have sent out depicts the lower man of each one fighting that which they believe to be their enemy, when in reality they are fighting the picture of their own lower selves. These pictures change the closest friends into enemies and array brother against brother.

"Should this band still persist in their threatened attack and raid, they will destroy each other. They now have the opportunity of leaving the district and its inhabitants unmolested or they will turn and destroy themselves. Man cannot attempt to destroy his brother without meeting the same fate for himself. We send only the pure white ray of God love to them and if they resist that love with hate, malice, or revenge, they, of their own free will, turn that ray into a flame that will consume them. You need have no fear. We offer only love and have no power to compel them to accept. If the bandits come with love, there will be no conflict. Our cause is already won."

At this juncture a call came that there was a messenger approaching the village. We went out to meet him. He told us that the bandits had discontinued their raids and were peacefully encamped about twenty miles from the Tau Cross and had not harmed any of the inhabitants or their possessions since the appeal for help, but that they were holding the prisoners as hostages against further resistance. He also said there was a persistent rumor that the band would attack our village within the next day or two if the treasure was not delivered the following day.

The messenger brought greetings from the captive people. Every man had offered his life for the protection of the village. The messenger was told that this sacrifice would not be necessary and that he could return with the thanks and deepest appreciation of the villagers for the proffered service.

CHAPTER IV

W E resumed our work next morning with renewed zest, having banished all fear from our thoughts. On the morning of the second day we were working on some of the figures carved in the rock of the canyon wall.

Suddenly our attention was drawn to the village sentry whose position was across the canyon at a greater elevation, affording a much wider outlook. Through our field glasses we saw him signal the village. Soon the villagers were hurrying to and fro evidently seeking protection in the great gorges deeper in the mountain fastness. All the inhabitants were deeply agitated.

As we listened we could hear the low thundering roar of the advancing horde. One of our party climbed to a higher position which gave a broader view of the situation. He called back, stating that he could see the cloud of dust raised by the horsemen as they advanced toward the entrance of the canyon. We secreted our equipment in a nearby crevasse, joined our associate and found shelter in the surrounding crags and rocks where we could observe the movements of the band. As they entered the canyon, the band halted; fifty horsemen rode forward as an advance guard, then the whole band moved up the canyon, spurring and lashing their horses into a wild gallop. The clatter and roar of the hoofs over the rocky floor, coupled with shouts of defiance, caused an indescribable din. Had it not been so tragic at the time, it would have been awe-inspiring to witness this great body of horsemen sweeping forward.

Our position was very advantageous, as the canyon walls were nearly precipitous so that we could look directly down upon the bandit horde as they swept on with the seemingly irresistible force of a great tidal wave.

The advance band of intruders had swept past our position and those in the lead of the main band were fast approaching. We had turned our field glasses on the little village for the moment and observed that it was panic-stricken.

One member of our party working on the ledge, stopped work and was watching the advancing band. We saw him turn and look through the door leading to the entrance of the center room of the Temple.

Our field glasses were all centered upon the figure of Jesus as He advanced through the door and stepped upon the ledge, walking directly to the brink and standing for a moment with body magnificently poised.

This ledge was about eight hundred feet above where we were concealed and nearly three miles distant. Instantly we realized that He was speaking, and, in another moment, the words came to us clear and distinct. Our associate on the ledge sat down and began taking notes in shorthand, which I did also. Later comparison showed that we heard His words distinctly above the din of the advancing hordes. We were told that He did not raise His voice above His natural well-modulated tones.

As Jesus began speaking, a perfect calm came over the entire village and its inhabitants. These are His words, translated into English by Jesus Himself. My most fervent prayer will always be that I shall never forget them, though I live to be ten thousand years.

THE LIGHT

"As I stand alone in Your great silence, God my Father, in the midst of me there blazes a pure light and it fills every atom of my whole being with its great radiance. Life, Love, Strength, Purity, Beauty, Perfection, stand forth in all dominion within me. As I gaze into the very heart of this light, I see another light,—liquid, soft, golden-white and radiantly luminous,—absorbing, mothering and giving forth the caressing fire of the Greater Light.

"Now I know that I am God and one with God's whole universe. I whisper to God my Father and I am undisturbed.

STILL IN THE SILENCE

"Yet in this complete silence there exists God's Greatest Activity. Again, I am undisturbed and complete silence is all about me. Now the radiance of this light spreads to God's vast universe and everywhere I know there is God's conscious life. Again, I say fearlessly, I am God; I am silent and unafraid.

"I lift the Christ high within me and sing God's praise. In the tones of my music inspiration hums. Louder and louder within me the Great Mother sings of new life. Louder and clearer with each new day, inspiration is lifting my conscious thought until it is attuned to God's rhythm. Again, I lift the Christ high and give close ear that I may hear the glad music. My keynote is harmony and the theme of my song is God and God seals my song as Truth.

BEHOLD I AM BORN ANEW, A
CHRIST IS HERE

"I am free with the great light of Your Spirit, God my Father, Your seal is placed upon my forehead. I accept.

40

"I hold your light high, God my Father. Again, I accept."

As Jesus ceased speaking, a dazzling ray of pure white light shot out from the center of the solar part of His body. This beam of light extended down the canyon some distance to where the gorge made an abrupt left turn, just ahead of the place where the advanced group of horsemen were riding.

At the point where this light beam terminated, a great barrier like a stone wall seemed to rise instantly; and great darts that appeared like flaming arrows shot out from this barrier.

The advancing horses stopped so suddenly in their mad forward dash that they unseated a number of their riders. Many of them paused for a moment with their heads and forefeet in the air, then turned and bolted down the canyon completely out of control. When they reached the advance ranks of the main band, those riders that had not been unseated attempted to control their horses but to no avail. These, as well as the riderless horses, plunged on and into the front ranks of the moving band. Here the movements of the front ranks were checked, while the ranks in the rear, not realizing their danger, came on and surged over those in advance, until the canyon below us was a seething mass of men and horses.

For an instant all was a dead calm save for the wild screams of frightened men and mad horses, where the wild stampede of the advance riders had clashed with the forward columns of the main band. There, a terrific scene was taking place. The riderless horses, entirely free from restraining hands, had plunged headlong into and over the advanced ranks, unseating many more men; and they with their ungoverned mounts, added to the confusion. The

41

horses began rearing, plunging, and screaming, as only dumb animals can, in a moment of uncontrolled and violent fright. This mad melee was communicated through the massed horde in the canyon below us.

Suddenly we saw men draw their short swords and slash wildly in every direction; others drew their firearms and began shooting at men and horses in an attempt to clear the way for an escape. It soon developed into a battle of the survival of the fit. It ended in a mad dash for liberty by those who were fortunate enough to escape the shambles, leaving the gorge cluttered with great heaps of dead and wounded men and horses.

We hurried down to give what aid we could to the wounded. All of the inhabitants and our friends joined us. Messengers were sent out far and wide for assistance. We worked feverishly through the night and till after sunup the next morning.

As rapidly as we were able to extricate the wounded ones from the terrible debris, Jesus and our friends would take them in hand. When the last man was cared for, we returned to the lodge for breakfast. Much to our surprise, as we entered, we found the Black Bandit talking to Emil. It was the first time that any of us were conscious that Emil had been present. He saw our look of wonderment and said, "That will keep until later."

After the meal was finished, we walked outside with the Chief and he told us that Emil and himself had come upon the man seriously wounded and unable to move, as he was held down by his fallen horse. They had freed him and carried him to the temporary shelter where he was made as comfortable as possible; then they had called our hostess and turned him over to her care. After his wounds were dressed, he asked if she would ask her God to show him what to do to be like her. He also asked her to teach him how to pray.

She asked him if he wished to be whole and well and he replied "Yes, wholly like you." She answered, "Now that you have asked for wholeness, your prayer is answered; you are completely whole now."

The man lapsed into a deep slumber. At midnight when our Chief made his rounds, he found that the wounds had completely closed and there was not a scar left. The man arose, dressed, and volunteered to assist in the rescue work.

We also saw a great number that we thought were just slipping into the great shadow, restored completely. Some would cringe in terror at the approach of our friends, — so much so, that it became necessary to separate them from the others.

After the rescue work was finished, the "Black One," as we called him, went about among his wounded associates, doing all he could to alleviate their fears. Many seemed like animals caught in a trap, fearing that a terrible death by torture awaited them, as that was the sentence meted out to them through the law of that land, should a bandit be captured. So definitely had this belief become fixed in their minds that they never responded to the kindness bestowed upon them. They feared they were being nurtured back to health so that the torture would be of greater duration.

All were finally healed of their wounds, although a few lingered for months, evidently thinking they were delaying the day of torture.

The Black One later organized all of the wounded who would join him into a protective unit against further raids and also induced many of the inhabitants to join this unit. From that time on, we were later informed, the bandit groups never again attempted to raid that district.

Later two of our expeditions passed through that territory on their way to the Gobi. This man with his followers conducted them safely through his own district and the adjoining district, a distance of over four hundred miles, and neither he nor his followers would accept any compensation for that service. We have been told many times that he has become a great power for good throughout the district, giving his entire life freely to the people without remuneration.

CHAPTER V

BY noon of the second day, the wounded had all been cared for and we made a last survey to make sure that there were no more wounded alive among the debris. On our way to the lodge for lunch and much-needed rest, one of the party voiced the thought which had been uppermost for hours in all our minds: Why this terrible holocaust, this destruction of life?

We were tired to the very marrow of our bones and were completely floored by the shock. The brunt of the rescue work, especially in the early hours, had fallen to our lot, as the inhabitants had stood in such mortal terror of these bandits that it was very difficult to persuade them to lend assistance even after we had freed many from the entangled horses.

The villagers could see no reason why they should assist in saving the lives of those who were attempting to take their lives. Many of them have a deep aversion to touching any dead thing. Had it not been for our friends, the inhabitants would have left the scene immediately, never to have returned. As it was, we were weary and heartsick, having undergone the most terrible experience of our whole lives.

We arrived at the lodge, refreshed ourselves and sat down at the table completely unnerved. Shortly the food began to appear. We were all alone, our Chief having accompanied one or two of our friends and Lin Chu, the Black One, on a trip down the valley. After the meal we retired to our rooms to rest and none of the party awoke till late the next afternoon.

While we were dressing, it was suggested that we

go directly to our sanctuary, as we called the upper room of the Temple. We left the lodge and started to walk to the Temple as had been the custom on previous occasions. We had proceeded to the ladder that led to the entrance of the tunnel, when the one who was in advance stopped, with one foot on the first rung, and said: "What has come over us? Just a day or two ago we were in the seventh heaven of delight, going from place to place at will and accomplishing things in three months that we had expected would take years to finish. Our food appears on the table, and all of this without the least exertion on our part. Now, suddenly, we have slumped back into our old habits. I want to know why this sudden slump? I can see only one thing. Every one of us has taken upon himself the condition of the experience through which we have passed. This is what is now hampering us and I for one am through with that thing, it is no part of me whatsoever. It is not mine only as I worship it and hold to it and do not let it go. I step forth out of this condition into a higher and better condition and let go. I am entirely through with it." As we stood and stared at him, we realized he was gone, he had disappeared.

We were nonplussed for the moment as we saw this man attain; yet none of us would let go of that which was holding us back, though knowing full well that we were still holding on to a condition that did not concern us in the least. Consequently, we were obliged to climb the ladder, go through the tunnel, then up through the different rooms to reach our objective. When we arrived, we found our associate already there.

As we were talking of the accomplishment, Jesus, the other friends, and our Chief appeared. They walked into the room through the door that opened on to the ledge. We sat down and Jesus began by saying: "There are so many declaring that they are the sons of God and that they have all that the Father has. They do have all the Father has, but this statement has not been made a fact until they have the courage to take the next step and see themselves as God—one with all that God is; then they do accomplish. When the one in mortal limited thought sees the Christ stand forth, that finer individuality does radiate light. That one that is projecting the Christ does see with a finer, clearer, and more extended vision. That one sees the higher body of himself vibrating at a higher rate than does his limited body that he also sees.

"He thinks that these are two bodies. He also thinks that that body is the Christ of another. These which appear two are only an appearance, because he does not believe that he is the Christ. Let this one declare himself the Christ and actually accept it as a fact; that instant, these two merge and that one has brought forth the Christ. Then the Christ stands forth triumphant. Now let him go one step further and declare that the Christ of God stands forth and that instant he is the Christ of God. Now the Son of God is one with God the Father and he does go directly to the Father. That one must go one more step. This is the greatest and takes the greatest determination, as every fear of mortal thought and limitation must be erased: he must step forth, go forth direct to God the source, or the Father, and declare definitely and know positively without fear of precedent or superstition, or man-made belief, that he is God; that he is merged wholly or amalgamated with God; that he is this Love, Wisdom, Understanding; that he is substance; that he is every attribute of God the Father, the source, the Principle. He must accept this in all humility—such as one does show forth God. Through such an one, every one of the

God attributes does flow out to the whole world. To that one, nothing is impossible. It is only through such a one that God can express. When you amalgamate yourself with God, nothing is impossible to you. You not only have all the Father has but you are all that the Father is. You are the trinity. You are man-Christ, Christ of God, GOD, all three in ONE. The Holy Spirit abides with you. The Whole-I-Spirit in creative action abides with you. When you accept this, then you, as well as all others, will sing ALL HAIL the power of the Christ name, not the name of Jesus the personal but the Christ. Let angels prostrate fall; bring forth the royal diadem and crown Christ Lord of all. You do not crown the personal Jesus, you crown Christ; and Christ deserves the most magnificent of all royal diadems in the Christly crown. There are no diadems too great or divine for the crown of the triumphant Christ. You see that whosoever will, may come. Come forth and become the triumphant Christ. Whosoever will, let them come.

"When you say, 'God,' see yourself as God. See God standing forth as you stand forth. God cannot be a bigot or a boaster or an egotist. Neither can the Christ, the God-man, the image and likeness of God, be any of these things. You can be just God and so is God-man. 'I AM is in the Father and the Father is in me,' are true words. I AM and my Father are ONE in all meekness and Almighty Greatness. God and all mankind united are Almighty—the Almightiness of God.

"That which was born in your so-called iniquitous thought is raised in glory because the thought of iniquity is erased. That which has borne the image of the earthly must and does bear the divine image when you raise up that ideal image.

"I say to you that now, this instant, is the great

opportunity for you to step forth, out of this outer turmoil, into the great peace and blessings of God, and clothe yourself with the light of God. In all meekness, place the crown of Christ upon your head and, unless you yourself do this, no other can place it there for you.

"Step up to and be a part of the great white throne, the source. Become one with those that have made the great accomplishment in like manner; be not only one with God but be God, actually GOD. Then you can and do present the divine attributes to the whole world. How can God-energy get into expression except through man? There is not another organism upon the whole earth that can vibrate at the same rate or frequency; and in consequence, it is so highly organized that it does perceive, then generate and transform this supreme energy, which enables man to express God to the whole world. How can this be done except through the highly organized and perfected body which are when you are in full control of that body?

"That control means full and complete Mastership, Messiahship, Discipleship. You are only in control of and in perfect harmony with this body when you stand forth in perfect dominion and mastery in all the attributes of the Holy Trinity.

"The I AM man, the Christ, the Christ of God; then combining these three with the highest, God, — you are GOD.

"This is you, the man of today (all humanity) extending your vision and perceiving the truth about yourselves, that there is a higher and better life for you than the round of mundane experiences. This you perceive as you follow the right-used (righteous) path, in harmony and true accord, with the highest ideals you can present, or look forward to or set forth in love, reverence, and worship.

"The first step, you, man, become the Christ man, the only begotten son of God. The next step, you become the Christ of God by seeing the Christ-man, the Christ of God. You have joined the Christ-man to the Christ of God; then, in order to go direct to the source, you must take these One, God the Father. You have now brought together the I AM man into the Christ-man; then you have transformed this Christ-man into the Christ of God, or the Lord God. Then, through your next step, you have transformed the Christ of God into the ever-living God. These which seemed two have become ONE God. God, the Father of all. There is not one thing that will be impossible to you if you do not deviate from this path of right-use-ness. In this you must be absolutely fearless and true, regardless of what the whole world may think. In standing forth and acknowledging your dominion and at-one-ment, you are at one with the Father, the outpouring and ever-present Supreme Principle of all things.

"With this light does not your Bible present a great allegorical depiction of man's spiritual development and attainment when rightly understood or righteously used?

"The shaft of light that is pictured as coming to me from heaven, is projected outwardly from my body. It is true that this light is from heaven, as heaven is all about us and is light vibration. The actual focal center or starting point of heaven must be right within my body. Therefore, this heavenly light must come forth from me. The I AM of me must allow this light essence to come in; then I must generate and transform this light energy so that it can be sent out with any density that God, the I AM, desires. When this is done, nothing can resist the power of this pure light. These are the beams or rays of light that you see emanating from my body when

the artist portrayed me at Gethsemane. The beams
of light went *out* from my body instead of coming
out of heaven to me.

"Just so can you transform God-power and send it
out with such force that it is irresistible. It is the
God-power, which is recognized all about you, allowed to come in, be generated and transformed
within your body, then sent out through the reflector.

"These things are readily accomplished by all
when they stand forth as God, their divine heritage,
the Christ of God, all One. This is the divine and
definite motto for all humanity.

"The closer humanity draws to this great healing
ray, the earlier will discord and inharmony be
erased.

"If you live freely in this light vibration which is
the light of the whole world, and all draw near to it,
the closer you will draw to man's true abiding-place.
Thus you find that I AM is the light of the whole
world. Behold God, the table is spread. Lift up this
mighty one of God, this I AM. Lift this body to God
and you and all are crowned Lord of All.

"You do place the crown upon your own head.
None can do this for you."

CHAPTER VI

MY only apology for dwelling in detail upon the experiences of these few days in regard to the bandits is to portray as conclusively as possible the power of one man clothed completely in his divine right of dominion and mastery, to turn the energy and zeal exerted and sent out by a great lawless horde to the complete protection of himself and the whole district.

This protection was not only afforded but the energy and zeal released by the horde was so great that when it was magnified, energized, and returned, it caused those that would destroy to turn upon and destroy themselves. It also afforded complete protection to the whole countryside for many miles around, although the inhabitants were outnumbered by the bandits at least three to one and they had no visible weapons of defense.

As soon as the excitement and the shock of the previous days had abated, we returned to our work with renewed interest. The Easter season was fast approaching and we wished to complete our work in this locality in order to return to India.

From this time on our work drew rapidly to a close. The last details preparatory to the return were completed the day before Easter. We looked forward to Easter Sunday as a day of complete rest and relaxation.

On our way to the Temple, long before dawn, we found Chander Sen seated in the garden. He arose to accompany us, saying that our Chief would meet us in the Sanctuary. He suggested that we return to India by way of Lhasa, thence to Muktinath through the Trans-Himalaya Pass to Kandernath, thence to Darjeeling. As we reached the foot of the ladder which led to the Temple entrance, we halted for a moment to view the approaching dawn.

Chander Sen placed one hand upon the ladder and stood as though about to ascend to the tunnel entrance.

In this attitude he began talking: "Light does not comprehend darkness, as it shines through darkness. When Jesus saw that he was to be betrayed by Judas, He said, 'Now is the Son of man glorified, and God is glorified in him.' The Master mind did not say, 'Judas betrayed me'; He did not refer to Judas at all. He understood and held only to the Allness of the glorified Christ of God flowing through Himself. Thus we see that perfect mutual action works out all inharmony in its own way. Now you can say, 'Christ, stand forth more and more definitely, so definite that you are myself.' In fact, now are we one body, one mind, one spirit; one whole, complete principle. You are I AM, I am, together we are God."

The moment he ceased speaking we were in our Sanctuary, the center room of the Tau Cross Temple. We had scarcely composed ourselves when Jesus and a number of others, including our Chief, entered the door that communicated with the ledge.

As they entered, a great burst of light filled the room. Greetings were exchanged and we were introduced to the stranger who entered with them. He appeared to be an elderly man, yet very vital. We were told that he was one of the Munis who had charge of the caves near Hastinapur. He was returning to that district and would accompany us. He had known the great Rishi Vegas and also had met Rishi Agastya whose hermitage is located in that most lovely yet secluded spot. We were overjoyed at our good fortune.

We formed a circle and, placing both hands, palms down, upon the table, stood in deep silence for a few moments. Although there was not a word uttered, the room was completely filled with a strange, pulsing, vibrating emanation. It was an entirely different sensation from anything we had ever experienced and at first seemed to overwhelm us. The rocks pulsated and vibrated with a resonant musical tone. This lasted only a few moments. When the stillness was broken we were told that this morning we would see the creation of a universe in pictures. These pictures would be a representation of that which happened when our universe came into existence.

We stepped through the door, out upon the ledge, and walked to the edge. It was still an hour before sunrise. The dead calm of the absolute silence enshrouded us. The time was propitious for the unfolding of another birth. We were looking out and out into infinite space, our souls eager and expectant.

The Muni began by saying, "There are but two events in the world: that which was in existence before consciousness began to assert itself, is now, and ever shall be; and the things that humanity has thought and will think about.

"That which was before consciousness began, is eternal; that which humanity thinks is changeable and inconstant; that which was, before consciousness began, is Truth; that which humanity thinks is truth, is truth to them. When the Law of Truth comes to consciousness, it will erase all that humanity has ever thought erroneously.

"As the centuries roll on and push back the material veil by the process of evolution, thoughts come through the mind of humanity that revert back to Truth or, as we call it, the original cosmic fact; and these thoughts that fill the memory of the past, faced with the facts of the present and overshadowed by prophecies of the future, stand out definitely upon the path of the whole evolving race consciousness. Thus the race is called back again and again to the original existing principle. By this return and repetition, humanity is shown that Creation is eternal, the same with all mankind; but mankind's creatures are always changing and they are under a manifestation of Law called action and reaction. When human beings have gone far enough in their creation of creatures, the Great Absolute Law of Truth takes a hand in bringing them face to face with the original plan. Thus we see that cosmic law never allows life to run too far in a tangent. This law is always polarized in equalization, balance, and harmony.

"In spite of idols or creeds it will crowd mankind on into complete union with Absolute Realities. All things that are not in perfect accord and union with actual, existing cosmic fact, must erase themselves when the Absolute Law of Truth holds sway in the human consciousness. The thoughts of humanity are always so formed as to release their imperfect creations, that are only born of half-truths, when Truth arrives.

"Cosmic Absolute Law must be fully satisfied. Thinking, speaking, or acting the Law of Reality is bound eventually to lead humanity into Law or Reality itself. The ancients tell us that every tree that the Heavenly Father has not planted within you, will be uprooted. 'Let them alone, blind leaders of the blind. If the blind always lead the blind, shall they not fall into the same ditch?'

"The cycle is fast closing in which the blind of the whole race have led the blind into a welter of ignorance, superstition, and delusion created by those who believe as human beings think, rather than that which is true and real. The civilization that has risen on the delusions and superstitions of the closing centuries is submerging itself in the welter. Through the pain and tragedy of their misappropriated creations, a new race consciousness has been conceived and is fast evolving. In fact, the door is opening wide for its new birth.

"There is no other course than to go on from one plane of consciousness to a higher and more advanced step in the actual cosmic path. The only condition forbidden in the vibration of the great cosmos is that quality of thought which allows the human race to become so solidly fixed in what it believes that, if it clings desperately to its old delusions and will not let go, it can in no way come into the greater expanse of universal thought. Those thus absorbed in personal consciousness must go on through natural exhaustion of beliefs and experiences until they fail to go forward; then, of its own accord, Absolute Law wields a progressive hand through disease, pain, and loss, until the human is satisfied and turns to find the curse of a false idea within the idea itself.

"If a race or nation refuses to let go of things created by a portion of human thought instead of that which really exists, the Law takes a hand in its progress by allowing the accumulated vibrations sent out by such a condition to reflect back upon itself through the light ray. Then with war, strife, discord, and death on every hand, that race or nation is wiped out, in order that it may be placed again in a new up-lift of creation. Thus it can begin over again in a new contact with that which was before the beginning of human consciousness. Civilization today is fast approaching a great reconstructive moment. All things that seem so stable and well-founded now will soon be immersed in a state of inversion. Every tree that has not been planted by Truth will be uprooted. There is approaching a complete cosmic

56

overthrow of the present social, political, financial, and religious institutions that will make room for the placing of the new era in order that humanity may come in closer touch with that which is and was established before the present human consciousness submerged and set it aside. Truth waits on with attentive, loving, and radiant beneficence until man will see that he can embrace and become the consciousness of that which has always existed.

"Humanity is taking a forward step from the cradle stories of the former generation and their creations are no longer of any avail to the arisen individuality and spiritual discernment of the consciousness of the generation that is fast approaching. Delusions, traditions, and superstitions are nearing the end. It is also true of the civilization which they established. The old idols are good enough for the infantile consciousness that is nearing an impasse. Their delusion has caused their undoing as they are proved to be only cradle stories woven by a master-craft of priesthood and preceptor to lull into false sleep the crying infants of an evolving race. Those who saw further afield did not cry and thus were not lulled to sleep. Most of them saw that the cradle stories were not true and many stepped boldly forth to erase the untruth; as they saw directly through to the Absolute, that which has always existed and which has always been seen and known and contacted directly by a portion of mankind. From this portion there will arise a new and more vitalizing consciousness, fully awake and ready to erase the idols that man has set up for his fellow man to follow and make room for the new ideals which are as old as creation's dawn.

"These will demand of those who teach, lead, or inspire the race-consciousness, that they shall do it from a plane of actual living contact, so high that there can be no mistake or contradiction and on a plane of interpretation that is so simple that it cannot be misunderstood. The awakening tiger of higher intelligence and spirituality will refuse to sleep again, as it is already ravaged with the fragments of the past and disappointed with the torture of misplaced confidence. It will demand a stronger and more vital thought with instruction based upon Truth itself.

"The multitudes are now listening, over the heads of past centuries with their creed-bound traditions, to the old, old message that to the newly-born is working its unfoldment into the hearts and lives of mankind. This new-old message is the clarion call that is heard above the changing voices of creed-bound priesthood. It is louder than the voice of battle; it is louder and clearer than the muffled contradictions of financial, industrial, political, and religious lies.

"In spite of the creed-bound thoughts of a portion of humanity, their traditional and idolized ideas of God, of Christ and man, of self, of life and death, all must go; and in the absolute freedom from these preconceived ideas there must pass and thus be erased all that was built upon them.

"There is looming upon the horizon of this new approach a redemption that has an entirely new meaning. This new multitude, coming out of this clearer vision and more definite perception, is redeemed through deeper revelation emanating out of all races and all people. That emanation is the One Life that is in all and through all.

"In spite of the delusion-bound multitude, their clinging hands and cringing attitude, a greater and more noble vista of the expanding horizon of God, the Christ of man, the Christ of God, of Self, and death itself, is looming; and another cycle of spirit is dawning for the whole world. Another age of the Crystal Race is coming up out of the maelstrom.

"Whenever a people or nation think of God as Absolute, that people or nation is God, for God is established unto them. As they love, worship, and reverence that ideal, they do become God. In the fullness of time they have reached their heritage, that which was first and is established in Spirit. Whenever an individual thinks of God, he is God, God is established unto him. Breathe life into humanity, it means the same, God. In this greater understanding of cosmic revelation, men find God the same as God was before human consciousness began to manifest — the same yesterday, today, and forever.

"There is slowly rising from the ashes of orthodoxy the actual temple not made by hands, eternal in heaven, in man. A great new race of thinkers is coming to the fore with herculean strides. Soon the tides will surge over the earth to sweep away the debris of delusion which has been strewn over the paths of those who are struggling along under the load of evolution.

"The work is already accomplished. Hundreds of millions are re-released with their heart, soul, body, and instinct free. They are the throbbing pulse of an unborn race that is again heir to the ages. I see them stepping across the ages, walking hand in hand with God. Great waves of wisdom flood toward them from the eternal shores of the infinite. They *dare* to step forth and declare themselves a part of eternal God, eternal Christ, — God and man One eternally with eternal life. They dare to step forth and declare to heaven that much that is written by man is a lie and in terrible blindness wrought.

"This new pulse-consciousness is the crest of the wave that rests on the new race-consciousness. This

new race sees man, himself, the highest expression
on this planet, and one with God through the medium of his life; and it sees that his whole supply
flows through that life itself. This race knows that
man can live consciously in a perfect universe with
perfect people and in perfect accord with perfect
situations and conditions, with absolute assurance
that there is not an error in the great Spiritual plan
of the Cosmos.

"Man sees God as Cosmic Spirit pervading everything; then, with the subtleties of mind through his
thought, he does not hesitate to review the funda-
mentals that have placed him where he is and made
him that which he is. Thus he is again one with his
sources. He knows that this source is the ever-silent
side of his God-mind linked consciously in thought
and amalgamated with Infinite Mind.

"This new race understands that, through sun and
shadow, without the bitterness, the soul's true quest
for Love and true Peace is the Truth of God and
man. This race does not hesitate to strip the swad-
dling clothes of delusion from the whole human
race. The gaunt specter which for ages has bound
the feet of the weak and doubting ego-man, through
his own ignorance, will be completely erased. He
finds he has erased his every limitation through his
true selfhood, completely arisen. He has raised himself from man, to God-man, to God."

CHAPTER VII

A FTER a short period of rest, as the first rays of
the sun came over the distant horizon, the Muni
stood up and said: "With me are those who
have learned many things which the Father sees for
humanity. They see with the comprehension of that
which penetrates Spirit; thus the whole wide world
comes under their vision. They see that which humanity feels. Thus they are able to assist humanity in
fulfilling its desires. They also hear thousands of
sounds usually inaudible, like the song of the humming bird, the sounds made by the newly-hatched
robin, the notes of the field cricket, some of which
sing at fifteen thousand vibrations a second, and
many other musical sounds far above the range of
the human ear.

"They are also able to feel, control, and send out
inaudible sounds that are capable of producing types
of emotional feelings such as love, peace, harmony,
and perfection that benefit the whole world.

"The vibrations of the feelings of abundance and
great joy can also be amplified and sent out by them
so that they surround and interpenetrate all humanity to such an extent that, if he will, each unit of the
human family may have them. When this condition
is acknowledged to exist, each human unit co-oper-
ates by amplifying and sending out these vibrations;
then, the very thing that humanity is in need of is
crystallized into form around or among its units, or
people. Their desires are accomplished. When the
necessary vibrations are set into activity, the units of
humanity can not escape the actual presence of

these. In this way, all of humanity's perfect desires are crystallized into actual form.

"The vast sea of God's creative, unlimited, moving space is crystal clear; yet it is completely full of vibrating, emanating energy; and that emanating energy is known as aqueous substance in which all substance or elements are in soluble form or suspended in harmonious relation, ready to respond to the call of the vibratory rate that will allow them to coalesce into form. When the proper vibratory influence is set up through the thoughts of the human unit, co-operating with the whole, the elements, having no other course, rush in and fill the mould set by the desire. This is absolute law and none can stay its true course.

"Listen. An organ is playing in very low bass notes. Now let us first lower these notes so that they are no longer audible to us. The feeling or emotion of the sound we have experienced still lingers, does it not? The vibration is going on just the same, although it is inaudible. Now let us carry these notes up and up through the scale until they are so high that they are again inaudible. The feeling or emotion still lingers; the higher vibration is going on just the same. We know that neither of the influences ever ceases although out of range of our physical ear.

"This is what we designate as Spirit. When the physical loses control, Spirit takes control; and that control is much more definite, as it has a much wider range of vibration than the mere physical and is much more susceptible to the control of thought-influences or vibrations, since thought is much closer allied to and co-ordinated with Spirit.

"The physical is limited to the body and does not extend from or away from it. The physical is limited, too, entirely to the actions of the body but not to its reactions. When it comes to body reactions we are

Spirit, if we define it as Spirit; thus you can see how the physical body is limited.

"Spirit not only penetrates every atom of the so-called physical, it also interpenetrates the minutest part of all substance, whether it be solid or gaseous. In fact, it is the force in which the mould is wrought that substance takes its various patterns from. In no other way can substance take its various forms. Man is the only projector and co-ordinator of these various patterns that substance assumes. Allow me to digress for a brief moment of explanation. You see the great central sun of our universe blazing forth in all its magnificent splendor and, as the horizon gradually withdraws and exposes to our view a new day, a new epoch, a new Easter is born.

"This so-called universe of ours that rotates around that central sun is but one of ninety-one such universes that rotate around a central sun. This sun is ninety-one thousand times larger than the whole or combined mass of all the ninety-one universes. This central sun is so colossal that each of the ninety-one universes, rotating around it in perfect order and sequence, is as small in comparison as the minute particles that spin around the central sun or nucleus of an atom, as you call it.

"It takes this universe over 26,800 years to accomplish one turn of its orbit around this great central sun. It moves in exact order with one complete precession of Polaris or the North Star. Do you doubt there is a great positive divine power controlling all? Let us return to our observations.

"Look closely. A picture is forming and on the film is the white globular disk of the sun. A spot of red is forming on the white disk. Now look more closely and you will see that a tiny point of pure white light has flashed out from the red disk. This is not a beam of light. It is a running point of pure light, the spark of life, emitted and included with that which is to be born. It is but a tiny point of light to you, yet it is huge to those who can view it at close range. How strange it seems to you. In a very short space of time, you will be looking through an instrument that assists your eye to see all these things. This will also reveal to humanity many more wonders.

"For millions of ages the great central sun has drawn to itself the throbbing, pulsating, yet harmonious emanations of energy which must give forth of itself or burst asunder. Observe that a great nebulous gaseous mass has burst forth from the sun. You have observed in pictures the birth of the planet Neptune, which is now a great mass of micro-cosmic particles or atoms that have been ejected from the parent sun with great force and power.

"While it is nebulous and indistinct, the point of light that appeared before the final expulsion took place is the central sun that has the power to attract to itself and hold together even the minutest particles as well as those of larger dimensions that have been given forth from the parent sun.

"Your first thought is that an explosion has taken place and that particles of the sun have been shot into space. Stop a moment and observe what has really happened. Why do the particles and gases cling close together and form a definite circular pattern? It is because of the intelligent Law back of and guiding it, in perfect order and harmony. This is proof that it is no accident but is in perfect order and sequence governed by Law, Law that never fails.

"This point of light or central nucleus is the central spark or son, the Christ of Humanity around which all humanity revolves. This is determined Spirit force. This Law prevails throughout all units of humanity. The central spark is a point of pure white light, the Christ which penetrated the *first* cell. Then it expands, divides, and gives off that light to another cell, which is born of its division but held together by a co-existing and cohesive force which is called LOVE.

"These particles are nourished and held together just as the mother holds and nourishes the child. It is in reality a child of the sun, which contains within itself the nucleus of central sun. That nucleus is the image and likeness of the parent that has just given it forth. As soon as it has come forth from the parent, this central sun has the same power to draw to itself, consolidate, and hold the vibrant emanating energy that surrounds it and which is necessary for its life and growth. It does finally consolidate the most extended orbit of our Universe.

"When Neptune first came forth and the central sun began to draw energy to itself, mostly from its parent, the sun, the atom began to consolidate into its form; that is, it began to shape itself into the pattern that was projected for it before its birth. It occupied what is known as the cradle orbit, the orbit within the orbit which Mercury occupies today. In this orbit, the child is able to draw its substance from the parent more successfully, as it is much nearer to the parent. As it drew substance from its parent, it began to consolidate into form. Instead of remaining mere gaseous vapors in the nebulous state, the chemical elements began to segregate and consolidate. The resultant solids from chemical action began to consolidate and rock structure began to form under intense heat and pressure. As this semi-liquid substance became more consolidated, it began to cool on the surface and a crust formed. This crust became heavier and more dense, both by the cooling process and by the assimilation of particles upon, and adding them to, the outside of the crust. When this crust became strong enough to hold the revolving mass together, this mass became the primary rock structure of the planet, with a semi-liquid molten mass at its center. Then, from the resultant gases and vapor, water began to appear as the product of the union of these gases. The nebula then became worthy of the name planet. It was now fast evolving toward a condition where it could sustain life; yet it must go on for eons of time, adding to its structure, particle by particle, from the outside. The continued cooling of the central mass brought it nearer and nearer to perfection, before its atmospheric, chemical conditions and surface were ready to bring forth life organisms and maintain those life organisms.

"At this juncture the parent sun began to give birth to another atom. As this expulsion was completed, Uranus was born. The extra force emitted with the expulsion threw Neptune out of its cradle or smaller orbit into a more extended one. It was compelled to take the orbit now occupied by Mercury, to make room in the cradle orbit for the newborn child, Uranus, in order that it might receive its nourishment from the parent until its nebulous structure became a planet.

"Again conditions settle down and go well for a long period of time. Neptune, the first child, is growing up and coming nearer to the conditions where it can support life. In fact, amoebic forms are appearing in its clouded, brackish water, or inland seas. Then another atom is ready to come forth and Saturn is born. The extra force given out at the time of this expulsion sends Uranus out of the cradle orbit and it also sends Neptune out of the orbit now occupied by the planet Venus.

"Neptune was now sufficiently cooled and its surface developed to a stage where it was able to support life. It was upon this planet, as it occupied this orbit, that the conditions for the support and nourishment of human life which the earth enjoys today were brought to the stage where the human life element could attach itself to the select amoeba necessary for the support and manifestation of the human form.

"Thus came into existence the first human race, not the animal amoeba, but the human amoeba, the amoeba of selective type and character, with intelligence that could and did shorten the process of evolution. Upon this planet conditions were perfect for selective human development and this development came on at a rapid pace.

"There were no lower animal organisms; thus animal life did not develop. The planet was occupied by superior human beings who rapidly developed into a perfect human race who were all able to supply and support themselves directly from Cosmic or Aqueous substance. Thus they would have been termed gods upon this earth. Many of the legends and myths of today have their inception in and are built around this great people. They were exactly like the principle that brought them into existence. This race, through their ability to express beauty and perfection, began to surround themselves with perfect and beautiful conditions; in fact, they built the planet into a paradise of beauty and perfection.

"It was intended that this race should forever maintain this perfect condition which they had accomplished by absolute control of all the elements. Thus, when they put forth a desire, it was fulfilled instantly.

"As time moved on, some began to evidence inactivity and selfishness in attempting to outdo their fellowman. This condition brought on divisions and divisions brought on selfishness and greed which caused dissensions. The time that should have been spent in creating for service and advancement was dissipated in strife and contention. Instead of holding closely to their source, they were differing and separating widely, until all but a few lost that which was high and noble. All but the few let go of their security and protection. This caused a vortex to gather around the planet.

"Instead of holding to the perfect patterns of the divine, whereby they could have accomplished a complete universe of divine attributes upon divine planets, they gave way to such an extent that when the next outburst occurred, it was so enormous that when the nebula was consolidated the resulting planet was larger in mass than all of those which had previously come forth. Thus the great planet Jupiter came forth. The excess energy given out was so gigantic that it swept Saturn out of the cradle orbit into the orbit now occupied by Mercury. The outburst was so tremendous and the solar system so filled that great quantities of asteroids formed, arrayed, and aligned themselves around Saturn. Being of a different polarity, they could not coalesce with Saturn; thus they were independent and their only alternative was to align themselves around the planet of Saturn as bands of asteroids. As such they are commonly called the rings of Saturn. Some of these asteroids are as large as planets.

"The force swept Neptune, the great and beautiful, out into the orbit now occupied by the Earth. All of its magnificence, with its great inhabitants, save a few, were swept away. Those who were preserved had never let go of their divine heritage and they had so constituted their bodies that they could seek safety in the emanations of the Spirit Sphere, which is all around and interpenetrates the ninety-one universes now in existence.

"In this condition they have been able to preserve

68

their identity and knowledge and give it out, so that it will never pass out of existence. It is through and by these ideals that we live today. We claim kinship with these great ones. They compose the root race of humanity. By them the ideals of humanity have been preserved and the Godhead of man has been maintained.

"Then followed many millions of eons of time needed for the nebula of Jupiter to take form as a planet. So enormous is its size that it has cooled but little even today.

"Time again passes on with swift wings and the sun is ready to give birth to the fifth nebula; and Mars, the blood-red planet, is brought into existtence. As this expulsion is complete, we see a phenomenon happening in mighty Jupiter. A huge red spot has suddenly developed on her side and she is expelling a great portion of herself; she has given birth to a satellite which is called a moon. There is such an excess of force set up as the two expulsions take place that the giant Jupiter is thrown out of the cradle orbit and room is made for the planet Mars.

"As the giant Jupiter occupies its new orbit, the whirling nebulous form is in no way able to gather to itself the great mass of particles that were expelled at the time of its birth. These particles were so far flung that they came within the influence of Neptune, Uranus, Saturn, and Mars; but, being of a different polarity, they could not be assimilated by those planets. They became separate asteroids without planetary polarity; thus they cannot take their place as planets and rotate in order and unison around the central sun. Consequently, they fly into space as vast swarms of meteors, with no rhythm of movement, speeding with fearful velocity, to collide with and imbed themselves in the surface of other planets or to be torn to pieces through the impact of collison.

"Also, in their mad rush through space, minute particles are carried away until they will gradually return to the aqueous mass, where they can be again taken up and assimilated by the great central sun, to be given off again as nebulae at the birth of other planets or atoms.

"Now comes the outburst that gives birth to the nebula that finally forms our Earth. Mars is thrown out of the cradle orbit and our Earth takes it place. Thus all of the planets are sent out into another orbit, to give space for the new child. Then Venus is born. In like manner the Earth and all other planets or atoms are thrown into ever-expanding orbits in order to make room in the cradle for the newborn planet or atom. Then Mercury is born, throwing the other planets or atoms into another widened orbit, making up the full complement of planets that are visible through astronomy today, eight in all.

"There are really nine, as the cradle orbit is not occupied by Mercury. It is occupied by the last nebula, or child, but that nebula has not consolidated into form so that it can be seen. It is there, nevertheless, and its influence is felt. Thus the universe that our earth is a part of contains nine planets or atoms with their nine orbits, which they follow in mathematical precision around the central sun or nucleus. You have been shown pictures of this creation as it came into being through orderly sequence.

"Something is happening to Neptune, the farthest removed planet from the sun, with the greatest orbit. It has reached maturity and also its limit in velocity. It has received its full light charge and is ready to come forth as a sun. It is going into decline as the new nebula begins to take form and the sun is ready to give birth to the tenth nebula. Before this expulsion takes place, Neptune has reached its limiting velocity in its spin around the central sun; it flies into space and explodes, then returns again to the aqueous. There it can again be taken up by the central sun, to add more energy to that sun, in order that more planets or atoms may come forth.

"In the universe of which our earth is a part, there can be but nine planets or particles spinning around the central sun at one time. Thus it is a constant round of birth, consolidation, then expansion, reaching the limiting velocity, flying off into space, exploding, disintegrating, then reassimilating by the sun in order to give forth new birth.

"Thus the sun is reassembling from the aqueous, that which it sends out to again become aqueous. It is a continuous renewal through regeneration into new birth. Were it not for this process, the great central sun of the ninety-one universes, as well as the central suns of the different universes, would have been consumed long ago and all would have returned to the Infinite in which all substances exist.

"A wise Intelligence that pervades all emanations and space calls the universes into form and starts them on their onward march. The sun or central nucleus never grows old nor dies. It accepts, absorbs, holds and consolidates, then gives birth to the atom; yet it never diminishes, as it is forever receiving and absorbing unto itself that which it is giving out. Thus regeneration and rebirth are going on all the time. Universes are being formed, expanding, and returning that which they have received. There is one round of progression from a low to a higher, then on to a higher attainment.

"The galaxy of ninety-one universes that our earth and its galaxy of planets or atoms are one part of, is but one galaxy in a still wider-flung universe of ninety-one galaxies that revolve around a still greater central nucleus or sun that has a mass ninety-one thousand times greater than the first galaxy mentioned. This condition goes on and repeats itself by ninety-one, almost indefinitely; the whole making up the great and infinite Cosmos, the galaxies that comprise the Milky Way, as you call it. This Cosmos is often called 'the Atomic Heat Ray,' the source of the sun's heat.

"This is not a cloud of stars in which your sun belongs. It is a nebula born or expelled from the great cosmic central sun or nucleus just mentioned. The sun, as you see it located in this nebula, is but a portion of the light rays from the sun; these particular rays are bent at an angle as they enter mass, then are reflected, until these bent and distorted rays make up the image of the sun and place it in a false position. These rays are reflected back so distinctly that you think you are actually looking at the sun. In like manner, many other planets or atoms are distorted by this phenomenon. Where there seem many, there are few in comparison; yet the total number of the actual is calculated in many millions.

"By looking at the picture closely, you will see that these nebulae or their suns are not disks but globular and round, flattened at the poles just as our earth is flattened. In looking at them, you are only observing the great flattened polar area.

"The stupendous mass of the great Cosmic sun exerts so profound an effect upon light rays that they are reflected completely around the Cosmos. They are also definitely affected and reflected by coming in contact with the Atomic or Cosmic rays and their particles are thrown out of place to such an extent that thousands of images of planets and stars are reflected from one collection. Thus thousands of planets and stars appear to be misplaced and many more thousands of the images are again reflected. When we look through the universe the images show both sides and we see the light that was released hundreds of millions of years before, which has made the complete round of the Cosmos. Thus we get two images instead of one.

"One image is of the planet as it was hundreds of thousands of years ago, while the other is as it was hundreds of millions of years ago. This follows through the whole great Cosmic order. In many instances we are actually looking at the great past and we can also see into the future by the same means.

"There is an invisible connection, like the thought or heart impulse amplified billions of cycles through which spiritual orders go forth, that controls all of the universes. These great throbbing impulses or heart throbs go out through the intelligence which pervades the Aqueous that surrounds the Cosmos which is its spiritual counterpart. It is these gigantic heart throbs that send the life currents into every atom of the complete Cosmos, and keep them moving in perfect order and rhythm. In this infinite Cosmos vastness, there can be no sick or discordant cells, as one sick or discordant cell would throw all out of unison. Then for a time chaos would result. This also pertains to the human organism when disturbed by discordant thought.

"It was from this central control that the term 'Godhead' was evolved. The heartbeat of the human unit corresponds to this heart throb, although in miniature.

"Man is from and is a counterpart of the intelligence which has control of the whole aqueous source. He is co-existent with the source and draws all direct from that great aqueous reservoir, just as the great central sun draws from that source, but in greater degree because of his union with the greater intelligence which is directing the source.

"Man, the unit of humanity, is a well-organized divine universe, though infinitesimal compared with the great whole of the universes. Yet man, as the unit of humanity, when he assumes and takes actual charge of his divinity, is most necessary, as he is of the great intelligence that is before and in control of the whole divine plan of all the universes. Thus, should all the universes be destroyed, man, in complete co-operation with primal intelligence which interpenetrates and pervades all emanations in the Aqueous as well as down to the lowliest physical forms, starting with light emanation, could rebuild all the universes. Should such a catastrophe occur, man not only has the power but is the power that does resolve himself back into primal intelligence wherein there is no destruction. When quiet again reigns and harmony is restored, it matters not to man, when he is back into primal intelligence, how many billions of ages pass to bring about primal perfection in order that the whole process may be started over again. Here man maintains oneness with infinity and can afford to wait until the time is ripe for the bringing forth of the universes. Then with the preserved consciousness of former experiences, he is better equipped to assist in the bringing forth of a more perfect and lasting condition. In this, man can never fail, as he is more definite than any form; and failure is not written in his horizon or in his consciousness.

"The infinitesimal becomes the infinite of all forms. When the wise sage says: 'I am deathless, ageless, eternal; there is not a thing in Life or light that I am not,' he is looking into and sees this vista. This is true divinity. The ascension is truly his."

CHAPTER VIII

W HEN the speaker closed, we realized that the sun was well past the meridian. We sat there, not spellbound, but enraptured, as we were actually enclosed in the vista that had been set before us.

Where had the horizon gone? We had dropped it entirely; we were in and of infinity. The infinite was ours for the reaching out and acceptance of it. Do you wonder? Could we grasp the magnitude of who we were, where we were, and the importance of our place in the great plan of the Cosmos? Not yet, dear friends, not yet. Would the world accept it? We did not know. We had looked into the long, long past. What the future portends we know not until we have proved it by actually living the present. What the past has been for millions of years we have seen.

We will look forward toward this accomplishment, knowing that the future extends as many millions of years as has been portrayed before us. We have dropped our old beliefs, forgiven them entirely, and we look forward to every accomplishment, not hopefully but knowing. The old beliefs, where are they? Gone, dispelled like a mist. The Cosmos stands forth crystal clear.

We were aware that the sun was shining but there was such a crystal brightness back of the sunlight that the sun seemed to darken.

We collected our notes and moved toward the entrance of our sanctuary. As we projected the impulse to take the step, we were traveling on beams of light rays. Thus we entered the room; yet there were no

limiting walls. The Cosmos still enraptured and enthralled us. Could it be that we were an intricate
part of this giganticity? The gigantic lies prostrate
before the grandeur of the surroundings.

We sat down and allowed the silence completely to
immerse us. Not a word was spoken. We were not
even conscious of the passing of time until someone
announced that the table was spread. The meal was
of keen momentary pleasure but the keynote of our
whole lives was the hours that had just passed. The
sun had again reached the horizon and was fast dis-
appearing as we arose from the table and walked out
upon the ledge.

What a vista lay before us! It was not sunset; it was
eternity, just a brief chapter being enacted for us,
and here were our dear friends living with it chapter
by chapter. Do you wonder that their lives are immortal? Do you wonder that we called them Masters?
Yet not a hint of this ever passed their lips. We
asked, "May we call you Masters?" Their answer was,
"Sons, we are but yourselves." Oh, the beauty, the
simplicity. Why can we not be as beautifully humble!

As we were preparing to leave the ledge, instead of
going down the stairs as we anticipated, we walked
to the brink. No sooner had we reached the edge
than we were all in the garden of the lodge. Not one
of our party was conscious of what had taken place.
We were not cognizant of going through the air or of
any movement at all. By this time we were so accustomed to surprises that we simply accepted the situation.

From the garden we walked to the village and
found that all was in readiness for an early start and
that a number of the villagers had left to break trail
through the snow that still blanketed the mountain
pass to a depth of ten or twelve feet. This pass was

about fifty miles from the village at an elevation of twelve thousand feet above sea level.

A large portion of the country is rugged and very difficult to travel over. It is the custom to pack the trail through the snow the day previous to its use so that the packed snow will freeze, thus supporting men and animals.

We arose long before dawn to find that every detail had been attended to. Jast and the Muni were to accompany us. The entire village had assembled to bid us Godspeed. We all regretted the necessity of leaving this village where we had spent two winters. We had formed a deep attachment for every one of the people there and knew that this feeling was reciprocated. They were simple, kindly folks. In order to show their appreciation, many went with us five or six miles. We exchanged our last farewells and were again on our way to India. Before we were actually to look down upon the southern slopes of the Himalayas, months would have elapsed.

As we walked along with the main body of the caravan, we became conscious that we were walking without effort. At times we seemed to see some point on the trail ahead, like a vision; the instant the point became definite, we were there, sometimes miles ahead of the main caravan.

At the noon hour, we found fires going and a meal prepared by three of the villagers who had stopped for this purpose. After lunch they returned to the village. We were told that the others had preceded us so that the trail through the snow over the summit would be easy to walk upon. Our camp was also ready for occupancy. All was prepared for us until we had crossed the pass and came down into the valley of Giama-nu-chu River; there we overtook the advance party of villagers. They had gone to all this

trouble in order that we might be assured safe conduct through the rugged mountainous country.
They left us here, as travel was easy through the
valley.

I am purposely introducing this brief description
to show, in a general way, the hospitality of these
simple, kindly people throughout the whole trip to
Lhasa. Seldom did we meet the cruel, austere native
of Tibet that so many travellers love to write about.

We followed down the valley of the Giama-nu-
chu, then up a tributary of that stream to the great
Tonjnor Jung pass, thence down the tributary of the
Tsan-Pu or Brahmaputra to Lhasa, where a welcome awaited us.

When we came within sight of the city, we felt we
were nearing a Taos pueblo. One could imagine
oneself standing before such a pueblo as we looked
around on all sides. The palace of the great Dalai
Lama or overlord of all Tibet stands out as the one
great jewel of the whole city. While this city is the
temporal head of Tibet, the deeper spiritual head is
the Living Buddha. He is supposed to rule spiritually
through the mysterious hidden city or center called
Shamballa, the celestial. To visit this sacred place
was one of our fondest hopes. It is supposed to be
buried deep under the sands of the Gobi.

We entered the city, accompanied by our escort,
and were conducted to our lodgings where our comfort had been provided for. A great crowd stood
around outside for hours to get a look at us, as white
people had seldom visited the city.

We were invited to go to the Monastery the next
morning at ten and were told that we must make our
every wish known, as all would deem it a special
pleasure to serve us. We had an escort wherever we
went and a guard was stationed at our door to keep
out the curious, as the inhabitants of Lhasa are

accustomed to walk into each others' homes unan-
nounced. We were the only diversion in their lives
and could not blame them for their expressions of
curiosity. If one of us went out alone they would
crowd around with the evident intention of finding
out whether or not we were real and sometimes this
inspection proved rather disconcerting for the recip-
ient of the inspection.

The next morning we were up early, completely
refreshed and prepared to go to the Monastery to
meet the High Priest who had preceded us only two
days. As we left the city with our guard, it looked as
if all of the inhabitants had turned out to do us
honor.

As we approached the Monastery, the High Priest
came out to meet us and, to our surprise, Emil and
his mother were with him.

It was a wonderful meeting. The Priest seemed
like a boy again, saying that he had wanted to see
Emil or some one of our friends. He felt that he had
failed in many things and wanted to talk to them in
order to get a more complete understanding.

He also gave us our first news of the little home
that had been erected in the village where he had
charge. We found him speaking English fluently and
very anxious to learn. We went to the Lamasery
where all were made comfortable. Turning to Emil's
mother the Priest said:

"Power is the demonstration of the active Principle of God, my Father. It is always the constructive
activity. There is never too much or too little of
God's perfect activity and manifestation; and God
never fails, is never inactive. God Principle is always
working constructively. I command that I do stand
forth and that I am in perfect harmony with the
active God Principle, and that alone."

Here Emil's mother took up the thought: "You

can go on still further and say just as definitely, 'I pour this divine flame through you, my physical body, and you are transmuted into that pure substance, which only God Principle sees.'

"Now it becomes necessary for you to accept and expand your consciousness to the God consciousness; and you, yourself, revel in God. You do actually become God, one with the Most High. Man belongs in this high estate. Here man is one with the essence of all things; he is truly God. Here no division can exist. Do you not see that man himself can become God or demon? Can you not see that man's true vibratory sphere is the whole vibratory sphere of God if he lives in that sphere? This is the only scientific sphere, the only place for man, and the only place where he can bring forth God and be one with God. Such a man is certainly more than the human concept of man.

"Do you not see then, that you belong to and are of God's Kingdom and not that of any demon which is created by man's own imaging faculty? Then, is it not a perfectly scientific and logical fact that man is and can be God or that he may image himself out of the God Kingdom and, therefore, create for himself a demoniacal realm which may seem real to him? I leave you to be the judge.

"This is the only issue upon which humanity stands or falls.

"There is but one choice, one purpose, one truth, and one science; and this makes you free. You become God or servants, as you choose.

"Stop for a moment and just think of the allness of God or Primal Cause, with no beginning or end, with universal scope, and surround yourself in this. As you become faithful and worship this, and this alone, ONE GOD, ONE ALMIGHTY PRESENCE — you will find that the vibrations of your body will change from the human to the God or Primal vibration. As you think, live, move, and become one with this vibration, you do worship; and what you worship, you idealize, you become. It is thus with and for all humanity. There is but one God, one Christ, One Union, One man; One general household, all brothers and sisters, all One.

"God cannot be brought forth as a person or a personal image but as an all-inclusive universality, interpenetrating all things. The moment you personalize, you idolize. Then you have the empty idol; you have lost the ideal. This ideal is not a dead saviour or a dead God. To make God alive and vital to you, you must think and know that you are God. This is more living and vital to you than anything. This is the divine science of your being. Then you, the Christ, your redeemer, becomes alive and one with you. You are that very thing. This becomes the motivating force of your whole life. You are redeeming yourself, the true you; you are one with God, truly God. By reverencing, loving, and worshipping this, it becomes ideal to you—God right within and active."

Here the talk drifted to the possibility of going to Shamballa. The Priest asked whether it would be possible for him to go. He was told that if he could lay aside the body and reassemble it again, he could go without difficulty and that the party would go that evening. It was arranged that they should meet at our lodge early in the evening and that our Chief should go with them. The party assembled shortly after our return. After a short talk, they left by the door and we did not see them again for a number of days.

During this time we were occupied in making measured drawings in the Monastery. One day we were rummaging in one of the basements of the old

Lamasery. After moving considerable debris, we came upon an old marble tablet. This we had carried out of doors and cleaned. When the cleansing was finished, the beauty of the carving and the exactness of the execution of detail surprised everyone. It even surprised the Lamas themselves.

An old Lama told us that when he was a very young boy he became a chela of one of the Grand Lamas who was in charge of the very old Lamasery at the time this tablet reposed in a niche in the wall and that his master insisted they visit this tablet the first Monday in each month at the hour of nine in the morning. He told us that as soon as they arrived at the niche where the tablet was placed and stood quiet for three or four minutes, a voice would sing the history of this tablet and the great things that the carvings portrayed.

The song claimed that the tablet was one of two that were carved to commemorate a great white civilization that had existed and flourished on a large portion of what is known as the American Continent, hundreds of thousands of years ago. The duplicate, or sister tablet, the song claimed, was in existence and could be found in the motherland of its creation, thus proving that such a land did exist.

We took the data as interpreted by the song. After a lapse of several years, we were working in the district described and found the twin or mate tablet imbedded in a great wall at the location claimed in the song. The walls proved to have been the walls of an old temple in Central America now in ruins. Thus it is seen how, through legend and song, direct truths are brought to light.

The interest we showed in the tablet and the legend repeated in the song gave us access to other records and data that were of invaluable assistance in our research work later. This incident was also the contributing factor that opened the doors to records that are in the Palace of the Dalai Lama, the Living Buddha, as well as those in the Monastery which have been guarded for hundreds of centuries. Many of these records and their importance were wholly unknown to those that guarded them. It was through legend in song that we were attracted to them, although with the exception of these tablets, they proved to be copies. These copies were carefully done and they pointed the way to the originals later on.

We were so completely engrossed in this work that we were unaware our friends and Chief had extended their stay. This we thought very little of, as unforeseen conditions can arise in this remote country to cause delays beyond our control. During this time the inhabitants had, in a measure, become accustomed to us and we had adjusted ourselves to their ways and means.

Curiosity had given way to friendliness on both sides and we were going about freely. The morning of the twelfth day, as we were preparing to go to the Monastery, we heard a commotion outside and, stepping out to investigate, we found that our friends had returned. Their trip had been successful and such a place as Shamballa did exist. We were told that much of the beauty and grandeur of its art and culture were still preserved in its original beauty and that its magnificence was beyond comparison.

CHAPTER IX

A T NOON of the next day, word was sent that the great Dalai Lama would receive us at the Palace. The High Priest came to our lodge that evening to instruct us in regard to the ceremonies. He was overjoyed that the audience had been granted without the usual delays. He told us that this privilege had been granted immediately upon the arrival of a messenger from Shamballa who had informed His Highness of the visit that had just been completed. He had also been informed of our experiences in the village where the little house had been erected.

We were anxious to make as good an impression as possible, as we were asking for concessions to carry on our work in the whole country. We were also told that the Bogodo Lama or Governor of the province would arrive before noon and had sent word by messenger that he would assist us all he could. This was a surprise indeed. It was quite evident that the next day would be an eventful one for our little party. We were up early and out with the reception party to meet the Governor.

He was very much pleased at this gesture and invited us to return with him as his guests. We accepted the invitation and when we arrived with the Governor, we were escorted to the guest chambers of the Palace. From there we went directly to the place where the first ceremonies were to be conducted preparatory to our being received at the Palace.

When we arrived, three Lamas sat enthroned on high carpeted chairs while others, of lesser rank, sat in the posture of Samadhi, upon the floor. Two Lamas in red plaited cloaks stood on high stools and led the incantations. Our friend, the High Priest or Abbot, sat on a throne shaded by a ceremonial umbrella, awaiting the Governor.

The great courtyard in the Lamasery yamen was most beautifully decorated for the occasion. The decorations represented scenes that took place in 1417. In these scenes Tsongkappa appeared on the stone altar of his Monastery. After addressing the multitude on the greatness of man's accomplishments, he became transfigured and disappeared with his body. He then returned and founded the Yellow Order or Reformed Established Church of Tibet, of which Lhasa is the central hub.

In a few moments the governor entered with his escort and advanced directly to the throne from which the Abbot had descended. They stood together to receive and conduct us to the audience chamber of the Dalai Lama. The great hall was decorated with gorgeous silk appliqué tapestries and yellow lacquered furniture.

Led by our escort, we knelt before His Highness for a moment, then arose and were conducted to seats. The Abbot, acting as spokesman, stated the object of our visit. His Highness arose and beckoned us to approach. An assistant conducted us to our respective places before the throne. The Abbot and the High Priest took their places at each end of the line, His Highness then descending from the throne and standing before us. He received a sceptre from the hands of one of the attendants and, walking before us, touched each one lightly on the forehead with the wand. With the High Priest acting as interpreter, he bade us welcome to Tibet, saying he was honored that we were his guests while in the city and that we should consider ourselves the honor guests of his country and people as long as we might remain and at any time when we should return to the country.

We asked many questions and were told that we should have his answer the next day. We were invited to inspect the records and tablets in the vaults of the palace. He called an attendant and gave several orders which were not translated for us, but we were informed that we were to have the liberty of the palace without restraint. His Highness gave us his blessing and, after a hearty handshake all around, we were conducted to our quarters, accompanied by the Abbot and the High Priest. They asked if they might come in, as they had many things to talk over.

The Priest began by saying: "We have had many remarkable things happen to us since you were with us in the little village. We have been looking over some of the tablets that are in our monastery and find they all refer to the older civilization that inhabited the Gobi. It is our thought that all civilizations and religious belief came from one source and, while we do not know the origin or date of the records, we are well satisfied that they are the thoughts of a people which lived many thousands of years ago. We have here a short synopsis of a translation that was made for us by a wandering Lama of the Kisu Abu and, with your permission, I will read it.

"We are fully aware of the fact that our religious thoughts of today originated about five thousand years ago, that they are only an admixture, so to speak, of the thoughts and beliefs of men who lived at that time. Some are myths, others are legends, and some are purely inspirational in character; yet none of them point to the highest possible attainment outlined, of the Christ of God being a part of the individual attainment, and the possibilities of attaining that goal through living a life that presents that ideal. How has it been possible for us to have escaped these things when they have been so long in our midst? I can readily see now that Buddha and all of the great and illumined ones taught thus. But how have we escaped the true import of their teachings for so long, living so near to them?

"We know that our beloved Tsongkappa attained to this degree by the life he lived. I know that others and the dear one you met today have gone far toward this accomplishment. I have seen him go and come at will; yet the people are priest-ridden, down-trodden, and miserable. Why is it that these things are submerged? Why are the people not taught to operate the great and only law, standing forth as that law? I can see that in this earlier civilization, each individual did actually know, abide by, and live, one with this law, this perfect condition. Any other manifestation depends wholly upon man and is the result of the ignorance of the law of perfection. It cannot be that this law is not thoroughly enough consolidated to be given to the whole human family. If this were true, it would not be law but a division of law which puts it back into nothing but a manifestation of law. Anything that is only a portion of a whole is but a manifestation of the whole, taken away from and consolidated unto itself, until it becomes an isolated atom with no polarity or connection with its source. Yet it flies around in space with a seeming orbit, only seeking, as it has no constituted orbit of its own. It only assumes the orbit of its source but never becomes one with the source.

"There are thousands of examples of this phenomenon today in our solar system, especially in regions between Jupiter and Mars. In this region, thousands of smaller bodies exist that seem to be related to the sun, as they follow a seeming path around the sun. They are only following the orbit of their parent Jupiter because of its attraction for them and their lack of polarity to the sun, their real source. They were expelled when Jupiter was expelled. They were never consolidated with Jupiter; still, they fly on and on with Jupiter, ignoring completely the sun, their real source. This we know conclusively is because of the lack of central polarization within themselves to the sun, their true source. Is Jupiter at fault in this case? Is the sun, the true parent, at fault; or is each tiny atom at fault? Is it not the same with humanity? Is the Father at fault? Is the fault with those who have the greater understanding or is the fault with those who have the lesser units of understanding? The fault must lie wholly within the lesser, as they refuse to become one with the greater."

Then turning to Emil, he said: "I can see since meeting you that it was wholly my fault that I clung to the lesser when the greater enveloped me wholly. But let us turn to the translation, as it is through this that I came to the vital turning point in my life.

"The great Cause, or Directive Principle, saw his son the Christ, the perfect man. He said, 'This is the Lord God, the Law of My Being to whom I have given dominion over heaven and earth and all that in them is; and this perfect One need not be in bondage to any mortal concept, as my Perfect Ideal is raised above any bondage and has the same power and dominion that I have. Thus, I speak through the Lord God of my Being.

"'It is not any command that I give unto you, except if you co-operate with Me in the Divine Creative Will, you will have no need for any other and you will set up no graven image before Me or yourself. Thus, you will not call images gods but you will know that you are God in whom I Am well pleased and you have the same dominion that I have. Now come close up to me, my son; amalgamate with me and I Am yourself and together we are God. Your body is the God-body which is idealized and which is in existence and was in existence before the human race was ever projected into form. This is humanity's being, God creation. All humanity have this perfect form and image if they will but accept this true image. This is the temple of God that belongs to man and is complete for man.

" 'You will not make any graven image or any likeness that is in heaven or earth or in the waters of the earth. You will not make any substance into any image or idol; for all creative substance is yours to use, pressed out to you in fullest measure. You will not bow down to any created things nor will you serve them; and thus there will not be any jealous thing, nor will there be any sin or any iniquity that may be visited upon any of your children unto any generation; for you will stand steadfast with your eyes always fixed upon the cause and, therefore, your ideal of that cause cannot diminish. Thus you will show forth the same love that I manifest for you.

" 'You will honor this Cause or Directive Principle, knowing that it is your Father and Mother and your days will be greater than the grains of sand upon the seashore which are without number.

" 'You will not wish to hurt or destroy or kill, for the creatures are your creations; they are your sons, your brothers, and you will love them as I do you.

" 'You will not commit adultery, as whatever you will have done unto these you will have done unto your father, your mother, your brother, your sister, or your loved one; for they are loved of the Cause as the Cause loves you.

"'You will not steal, for you but steal from the Cause; and if you steal from the Cause, you but steal from yourself.

"'You will not bear false witness against any creation, for in so doing, you bear false witness against the Cause which is yourself.

"'You will not covet anything, for in so doing, you but covet the Cause which is yourself; by holding yourself one with the Cause you have that which is perfect and is truly yours.

"'Thus you will not make images of silver or gold to worship as gods but, seeing yourself as one with all things pure, you are always pure.

"'Then you will not fear, for no God, save yourself will come to prove you; as you will know that the Cause—not personal but impersonal—is for all and fully envelops all.

"'Then you will erect an altar and on that altar you will build and always keep burning the undying fire, not of gods, but of the Directive Principle which is God. You behold yourself, the Christ, the perfect, the only begotten of the True Principle or Cause.

"'Knowing this fully, you may speak forth the word (GOD) and that word becomes visible. You are the creative and the Creator, around, above, below, within, One with the Divine Directive Principle-Cause, GOD.

"'The heavens obey God's voice, the silent voice of G O D speaking through man. God speaks. Man speaks. God always speaks through man. Thus when man speaks, God speaks.'"

The Priest resumed: "In connection with this I have worked out the following, which has given me a more definite outlook. This has also shown me that I must be definite in every thought, word, and deed and that I must live one with this definite principle. First picturing, in thought, word, and deed, I find I

90

am actually that very thing. I have taken the form of
the ideal I have expressed.

"During the darkest hour I know that God is.
During the times that I am afraid, I trust more definitely in God, my Father, right within. I rest quietly
in this assurance, knowing fully that all is well and
that my perfection is complete and finished now.

"I recognize God as the all-inclusive mind, my
Father, and I know fully that man is the Christ of
God, the image and likeness of God, my Father; the
source and I are ONE.

"Slowly but surely the day of absolute spiritual
vision approaches. It is here the moment I recognize
it. It is here now, full and complete. I praise and
bless the absolute spiritual vision. I thank you, Father, that it is fulfilling my highest ideal now.

"In working, I must always be conscious that I am
working in accord with God's conscious and never-
failing law.

"I now understand the words 'My peace I give unto
you, my love I give unto you, not as the world giveth,
give I unto you.'

"I also know the meaning of 'Build me a temple
within, that I AM may dwell therein among you.'
Then I AM is your God and you are as I AM. This
does not refer to any church or church organization.
It is the true temple of peace within man, where
God, the source of all things, actually dwells. Mankind built a tabernacle in which they could come together to worship the true ideal, the I AM, within,
this inner temple, which God and man hold for all.
The tabernacle was soon worshipped, the empty idol
created, the church as it exists today.

"When I hold to the true ideal, I hear my own
inner God-voice; and the revelation of that voice
supplies comfort, inspiration, and guidance in my
work in life. Even when two or three are gathered

together in my name, there I AM is always in the midst of them. How true are these words, for I AM is always within man.

"I wish to progress, I must work and stick to it, — never falter nor be cast down. I am the Christ, the ideal of God, in whom the Father is well pleased, the only begotten of God, the Father.

"I am the only one who knows, sees, and cooperates with the Father; the only offspring that God knows — and God knows all — for all can claim: 'IT IS FINISHED.'"

CHAPTER X

THE next morning as we were waiting for the Abbot, a messenger announced that we were expected to appear before the Dalai Lama at two o'clock that afternoon. Thereupon we went in search of the Abbot and located him as he was leaving the audience chamber.

His face was beaming, as he held in his hand our commission to enter the country at will. After reading the order which the messenger had brought us, he said, "This is not an order; it is only a request. The audience is called to confer upon you this commission." As we were all together, it was suggested that we go immediately to see the records. We proceeded thence in a group.

Upon our arrival a great surprise awaited us. There were thousands of clay tablets and records on copper and bronze plates, also beautifully carved tablets on thin white marble. As this was our first opportunity to contact this class of record, we decided to look them over at once.

The Abbot told us he was not familiar with the tablets but had been told that they were of Persian origin and that he would attempt to find a Lama who was familiar with them. Thereupon he departed and we began to look them over. The characters were not familiar to any of our party.

The tablets were made of two slabs of pure white marble about one quarter of an inch thick, put together like veneer with a cement that we could not identify. The edges were beautifully beveled and around each tablet was a margin of two inches with carved raised figures. Many of these figures were of pure gold inlay, while all the titles were of pure gold inlay but not raised. The tablets were carefully numbered by sets and a serial number given to each set. The dates were represented by wreaths of flowers intertwined with vines and leaves. If we were to record a date like January 1, 1894, the first month of the year would be represented by the stem of a flower not yet come into bud, inlaid with pure jade. The first day of the month would be represented by the stem just coming into bud, inlaid with gold. The 1 of 18, would be represented by the stem with the bud just opened enough to disclose the pistil of the flower. The petals of the flower are lapiz lazuli inlay, the pistil being gold inlay with a small diamond set in gold.

The 8 is the flower in full bloom with eight stamens showing, each stamen an inlay of gold around the pistil, with a smaller diamond set in the gold inlay.

The 9 is represented by a rose with nine petals in full bloom, one petal an inlay of lapiz lazuli, one of jade, and one of chalcedony; this order repeated three times. This shows that the last or the end of the digits was reached. Thus they used from 0 to 9, then repeated.

The 4 is a lily in the process of opening, with the pistil and three stamens showing. The bowl of the lily is an inlay of pale jade, the stamens are fire opal set with four small diamonds, and the pistil is of lapis lazuli inlay, set with four small diamonds.

The space given over to the text is outlined with a threadlike vine, inlaid with gold, the leaves being inlays of green jade, and everything being worked out in perfect detail. Every tablet is a perfect jewel in itself. The type of tablet and the method of dating would indicate early Atlantean. Each tablet would be worth a king's ransom, were they offered for sale.

As we were musing, the Abbot and Priest came up, accompanied by the old Lama who had charge of the records. We became so engrossed with his recital of the history that it was necessary for the Abbot to call our attention to the fact that the time for our appearance before the Dalai Lama was fast approaching and that we should be in robes ere this.

When we arrived at our quarters, we found robes laid out for each of us, but how to put them on was a facer to us. The time was passing so swiftly that we decided to make a bold quick try and put them on helter-skelter. It developed later on that some of them were inside out and others backside foremost, while a few had the robes on as they should be.

Upon arriving at the audience chamber, we beheld the Dalai Lama crossing the hall with his guard, to enter the chamber by the great doors. We were certain we saw a broad smile flit across his face.

We composed ourselves at attention to await the opening of the side door, which was our cue to enter the chamber. Soon the door opened and we were ushered in, amidst the most gorgeous decorations that it had been our lot to witness.

The ceiling of the room terminated in a great dome in the center. In this dome were three large openings through which great beams of sunlight flooded, lighting up the room with a brilliance and splendor too magnificent for description.

The walls were completely covered with gold-thread tapestries, interlaced with figures made of silver threads. In the center of the room, on a raised dais covered with a cloth of spun gold, sat the Dalai Lama, dressed in a robe of spun gold trimmed with purple and spun-silver cloth.

We were conducted before the Dalai Lama by the Abbot and the High Priest and, as before, they stood at either end of the line. After a word of greeting, the Dalai Lama stepped down from the dais and stood before us. He raised his hands; we knelt and received his blessing.

As we arose, he stepped to our Chief and, placing a brooch upon his breast, spoke through the interpreter, "This will allow you and your associates the freedom of this land. You may come and go at will and with it I bestow upon you this commission, which entitles you to the rank of a citizen of Tibet. I confer upon you the title of Lord of the Great Gobi." He then walked down the whole line, placed a smaller but similar brooch upon the breast of each one of the company. "Wear this as a token of my esteem. It will admit you to the whole land of Tibet. It is your password wherever you go." He took the scroll containing the commission from the hand of the Abbot and handed it to our Chief.

The brooches were beautifully made of gold, wrought in filigree with a most lifelike likeness of the Dalai Lama carved in relief on jade, set like a cameo in the center. To us, it was a jewel which we prize very highly. The Dalai Lama and all were graciousness itself. All we could say was, "Thank you."

The old Lama who had charge of the records was ushered in and we were informed that we would share the evening meal with the Dalai Lama.

After the meal was finished, the conversation drifted to the remarkable tablets. The Dalai Lama, as well as the old Lama, speaking through an interpreter, gave us a detailed account of the history of the tablets, all of which we carefully noted.

It seems that these tablets were discovered by a wandering Buddhist priest in the vaults under the ruins of an old temple in Persia. This priest stated that he was led to them by the sweet song he heard emanating from the ruins as he sat in Samadhi. The songs were so sweet and the voice so clear that he finally became interested, following in the direction from whence they came, and found himself within the ruined vault. The voice seemed to come from below. After a thorough inspection, he could find no evidence of an opening; so he determined to locate the source of the voice.

Securing crude tools, he began digging in the debris and discovered a flagstone that seemed to be only a portion of the floor of the ruined vault. His heart sank in despair, as he thought for a time that he had been led from the right path by the whistling through the old ruins.

Before leaving the place, he sat in meditation for a few moments and, as he sat thus, the voice became more clear and distinct, ending with the injunction to proceed. With almost superhuman effort he succeeded in removing the large flagstone. This disclosed an opening leading downward. As soon as he stepped through the opening into the passage, it was lighted up as by an unseen force. Ahead of him gleamed a bright light. He followed the light, which led him to the opening of a large vault, closed by huge stone doors. As he stood for a moment before these doors, the hinges began to creak and the great stone slab swung slowly, revealing an opening through which he passed. As he crossed the threshold, the voice rang out clear and sweet as though the owner occupied the interior. The light that seemed stationary at the doors, moved to the center of the great vault, lighting it fully. There in niches, in the walls of this vault, covered with dust and the accumulation of ages, were the tablets.

He inspected a few, realizing their beauty and value, then decided to wait until he could communicate with two or three of his trusted associates, and confer with them regarding the removal of the tablets to a place of safety. He left the vault, replaced the slab and covered it over again with the debris; then started on a quest for associates who would believe his story and who had the fortitude and means to carry out his plan.

This quest lasted for over three years. Nearly all those to whom he related his story thought he had gone stark mad. Finally, one day while on a pilgrimage, he came across three priests whom he had known while on a similar pilgrimage and he told them the story. At first, they were very skeptical but one evening at exactly nine, as they were sitting around the campfire, the voice began to sing of these records. The next day the four of them dropped out of the company and started the journey to the ruins. From that time on, at nine o'clock in the evening, the voice would sing. If they were weary and downcast, the voice would sing all the sweeter.

At the journey's end, as they were approaching the ruins, an hour before midday, a slight boyish form appeared before them and began singing, leading the way to the ruins. When they arrived, the flagstone was lifted and they went immediately to the vault. As they approached, the doors swung open and they entered. A short examination convinced the priests of the value and truth of the discovery. Indeed, so enraptured were they that they did not sleep for three days. They made all haste to a village about seventy miles distant to secure camels and supplies which would enable them to move the tablets to a place of greater safety.

They finally secured twelve camels, loaded them,

and returned. The tablets were packed in such a manner that they would not be injured. Securing three more camels, they started the long journey through Persia and Afghanistan to Peshawar.

Near Peshawar they secreted their burdens in a secluded cave, where they remained for five years. One of the priests always sat in Samadhi before the cave all the time, to protect the tablets. From Peshawar they were removed to Lahnda in Punjabi. Here they reposed for ten years. Then by slow stages, they were brought here and deposited in the palace of the Grand Lama. This took more than forty years to accomplish.

From this palace, they were to be taken to Shamballa. In other words, we had found them in transit.

At this time in the narrative, an attendant brought four of the tablets into the room and placed them carefully on the raised place that answered as a table around which we sat, so that we faced them. Just as the hands of the clock pointed to the hour of nine, a voice came forth in lilting tones, infinitely sweet, yet of a highly pitched immature boyish treble.

These are the words translated into English as faithfully as we are able to present them:

"That there is an all-wise, intelligent Spirit, that this intelligence is Divine and infinite and permeates all things, cannot be contradicted. Because this intelligence does permeate all things it is infinite and is the source of all. It is Divine and its Divinity brought into thinkable or visible form, the fact or truth of all things.

"You can name this all-wise, intelligent Spirit, God or Good, or what you will, as man must have a name for everything. Once he has named a thing, he has power to bring it into existence. If man names anything through true reverence, worship, and praise, he can and does become that which he names.

"Thus you can see that man by choice can become God or animal. He becomes the ideal which he presents for himself to follow. With this line of thinking, it is simple to see that man is the only-begotten Son of God, or the only-begotten son of the animal. Thus, by choice, man can become evil or devil if his eye beholds evil; or he becomes God, if his eye beholds God.

"In the formless state, the all-wise, intelligent Spirit was silent and contemplative; yet the intelligence was there and saw itself as the producer as well as the spectator of all animate and inanimate things. In this silent state, the all-wise, intelligent Spirit saw there was no modification; and resolving to emanate or bring forth the universe, this intelligence formed a picture of what the universe should be. Having naught but the perfect picture or Divine plan to follow, the universe willingly took the form directed by the intelligence.

"The Divine Ideal picture was expanded until it came into perfect visibility. This is the Universe that we see today, that is going on with the perfect plan held forth for it to assume.

"This Intelligence is and always has been the perceiver and director of its perfect, Divine Ideal plan.

"This Intelligence knew that it was necessary to bring forth animate form and endow it with all potentialities, through which it could express fully. This is what is known as immortal man. This Divine Ideal, which differentiates itself in all phases and directions, is the immortal of each man today. As this man was created in the Divine Ideal of all-wise Intelligence, Spirit, he was set forth as the Son of the Principle, with dominion over every attribute and every condition. Son means union with, not a servant of. It was necessary that this Son be wholly free to choose and in no way become a slave or a puppet.

"This immortal ideal must always include a portion or spark of the central fire of that which brought or projected it into existence. This projection was the first cell that finally became man's body and is the spark of life that always endures and never dies. This cell is, in name, the Christ. This cell, although divided and repeated many millions of times, retains the image of the Divine Spirit projected and implanted in it and cannot be perverted by man's thinking. Thus man is always Divine.

"This cell projects its divinity into every cell created by the multiplication of itself, *unless* perverted by man's thinking. The collection of these cells finally assumes unto itself a container or cover, which is called the human body. The spirit or essence, still in unmodified form, has the intelligence to see all changes going on around it. By always standing in his high dominion, man is Spirit and Spirit is God.

"This higher self must be thought of, pondered over, worshipped, and blessed as being right within man.

"First, there must be faith that it is there. This brings forth the knowing that it does exist in man; then the blessings and thanks given bring it into visibility. Man is that very thing itself. This is the way to the attainment of all knowledge.

"The brain at first seems to be the perceiver, because it is the aggregation of the more delicate cells; and these cells first accept the vibrations and amplify them so that they may be perceived by man. Then they are selected and sent to all the other organs; and each, if held in divine order, goes to the very organ to which it belongs.

"Each organ and nerve center is the seat or special

amplifying center for centralizing the real man. When they are harmonized and coordinated, man stands forth in all dominion and power. He has brought forth the Holy Ghost, the whole of the all-wise, intelligent Spirit in creative action. This is soul and body brought to one focal center. No man ever accomplishes anything unless he consciously or unconsciously brings every faculty to this one center. This is the place of power, the Christ within man, the place where man stands supreme.

"Then how can man suffer discord, inharmony, sin, or sickness unless he idealizes them and brings them into existence? If he stands forth always and at all times, as the all-wise, intelligent Spirit and knows no other, he cannot be conscious of anything less. With this highest ideal always held in the clear waters of man's intelligent thinking, he becomes God. He is certain to be answered by this inner voice at all times.

"Back of will, stands desire. Will, in its true estate, is a pure colorless force and is moved into action by desire. If there is no color or direction given to will, it is inactive. Place the desire in harmony with the will force and it will spring into action immediately and call legions to carry out its commands — the only requirement being that the commands are in Divine order.

"There are myriads of worlds. There is but one thought out of which they grew. Its law is order which cannot swerve. Its creatures are free to choose. Only they can create disorder, which in itself is pain and woe, hate, and fear. These, they alone can bring forth.

"The Great Principle stands forth as a Golden Light. It is not remote, it is right within yourself. Hold yourself within its glow and you will behold all things clearly.

"First, with all your being, know one thing: that your own thought when you stand, is one with that thought which brought forth the worlds.

"Out of the blackness of disorder and its outpouring of human misery, there must arise the order which is peace. When man learns that he is one with the thought which is of itself all beauty, all power, and all repose, he will know that his brother cannot rob him of his heart's desire. He will stand in the Light and draw unto himself his own.

"Let pass through your mind, my son, only the image you desire, which is Truth. Meditate only upon the true desire of your heart, knowing that it does not wrong any man and is most noble. Now it takes earthly form and is yours. This is the law through which you bring forth your heart's desire.

"Let him who puts forth his hand to draw the lightning to his brother recall that through his own soul and body will pass the bolt."

With further research, these tablets may prove to be copies of former records made to preserve the originals. If copies, they must have been made during the early Indo-Aryan Age. As far as is known, there is nothing like them in existence today. From what source but the One did they spring? Thus they could be repeated in song and verse many thousands of times.

Oh man, where is your crown?
From eternity it passes on.
Where is your soul! but from
The Infinite it grew
Forever and forever
Is it but select to you.

Here were the four tablets set before us, each one worth a King's ransom.

CHAPTER XI

I TRUST my readers will pardon the liberties I have taken in digressing from the main text. This has seemed necessary in order to get before you, in as concise a way as possible, a few of the numerous and widespread places where records have been found that refer directly to the older civilizations, their arts and culture, as well as the determining thoughts and motives which have maintained civilizations in very high accomplishments.

A few groups still achieve these higher accomplishments. These groups do in a measure, through the presentation of these achievements, become a guiding beacon for the human race as it again marches on to another high point in civilization's progress. It is still to be determined whether the mistakes of a few, accepted by the majority, can again overwhelm and carry the great bulk into oblivion for a great cycle of time.

It is our vision that the present holds all the future; nothing save the accomplishments of the present give form to the future. Thus humanity has but one road; if the present be made perfect, the future must be perfect. It is not the present perfection DELAYED to some future perfection, it is the conscious present perfection that brings forth the consciousness of the perfect future.

Wherever we go, we find a people that had, at one time, lived wholly in the present. The whole future was in complete accord with the attainments of the present, so the future could take no other direction. Thus the injunction, "Take no heed for the future."

All their precepts were, "Live true in the present and the future must be what the present has been."

Their folklore, their songs, their prayers—even those written on wheels—portray this thought. The devil dance, in which the Tibetan participated so freely, was originated to frighten away the evil one who had destroyed their race concept or consciousness. Through use, it has degenerated into a mere ceremony to frighten away evil spirits. The people have become so engrossed in spirits that they have forgotten the all-inclusive spiritual.

This is not confined to just one race or one creed but to all races and creeds. The first dance portrayed beauty and purity so thoroughly enthroned that not even a suggestion of evil could dethrone it.

We also investigated the goblin tales from the "sea of sand" as the Gobi is called in China. In many places one hears strange voices: many times we have heard our own names called. We have heard the din made by great throngs of people which seemed to be close by. Often we heard a variety of musical instruments accompanying sweet voices in song. We have seen many mirages and heard the noises of shifting sands.

We are certain that the air strata at some distance above the desert are so clarified that, at certain times, when all conditions are in harmonious accord, they act as sounding boards which reflect the vibrations that have at one time gone out. In this way we believe medieval happenings are reproduced through the vibrations that were sent out. Thus the air strata become the sounding boards that pick up and reflect the vibrations just as they pick up and send out the vibrations of a mirage.

We became so engrossed in our work that time seemed to have wings. Working under the direction of the old Lama, we made copies and measured drawings of many of the tablets as well as of other records.

The morning of our departure dawned bright and clear. We had paid our respects to all in the palace of the Dalai Lama; yet the streets were jammed with people, so anxious were they to wish us God speed. Everywhere hands were waving farewell or offering prayers for our safe conduct. A delegation preceded us for miles with prayer wheels on long poles, turning out prayers. Fifty accompanied us to Shigatze on the upper reaches of the Brahmaputra River. As we neared this, the second city in Tibet, the great Tashi-lunpo Lamasery, located a mile from the city, came into view. A delegation from this Lamasery met us three miles out and invited us to be the guests of the Lamasery during our stay. We were accorded a cordial welcome on every hand.

As we entered the Lamasery, we felt the calm and peace which pervaded its halls, as of a great presence. It was indeed an ideal place in which to rest before resuming our trek to Lake Dolma and Sansrawar. We were also anxious to inspect the records of this monastery. From there we wished to go on as rapidly as possible, as arrangements had been made to meet the Master Bhagavanzi at the Temple Poratat-sanga.

After the evening meal with the Lamas, we talked of the many beautiful temples. The conversation then drifted to the difference in religious beliefs. One very old Lama said: "The same beliefs are not shared by Lamas and Yogis. The Yogi cannot believe that the teaching of any one man can be final; he sees that every human being has access to all knowledge right within himself, while Lamas are adherents of Buddha alone. In all probability, each human being will unfold and realize his mightiness. A

Christian will reach the Christ consciousness, a Buddhist will reach the Buddha attainment, and so on. All have their gods and on every hand one can hear that God made man in his image. All nations and all peoples have their different gods.

"Some have their god of fire, others the god of harvest, and so on. Each has a better God than his brother. How am I to understand that God made man in his image, unless from the many gods set up, I would say that each man has made God in his, man's, own image?"

We found six Lamas at the head of a group that were known as the wandering Lamas, who go hither and yon without purse or scrip. They never beg, ask alms, or accept food or money from any one. They are always in touch with each other and with the six that are at the monastery. Of this order, there are three branches, with one at the head of each branch, making nine that are in charge. The three heads of the branches may be located in three different countries. Each of those who go out keeps in direct touch with the head of the branch he is working under; the head of the branch keeps in touch with the six. The method which they use for communication we call thought transference, for want of a better name, but we know it to be a force far more subtle and much more definite. They call it Atma, soul conversing with soul, using no other medium. We met six of these Lamas and had lunch with them the next day.

The old Lama informed us that he would accompany us to the Pora-tat-sanga temple when our work was finished. We accepted his offer, as he was a friend of the Muni who was acting as our guide and interpreter. They both assisted us in every way with the records.

During a conversation, the old Lama casually remarked: "Two of your associates who left you last summer will arrive in Calcutta at one-thirty today; and, if you wish to communicate with them, you can do so." Our Chief wrote a message instructing them to go directly to Darjeeling and look after a business matter which needed attention, and to await our arrival on August 24th. He dated the note, made a copy of it, and handed the original to the Lama. The Lama read the note, folded the paper carefully, and put it away.

Our associates did meet us in Darjeeling on the 24th of August. They showed us a written message which was placed in their hands not twenty minutes after their arrival in Calcutta. They supposed the man was a messenger who had been sent ahead with the message. Now we had physical proof of the ability of some of these Lamas. If this ability could be extended in one direction, why not in all directions?

We were anxious to press on toward Pora-tat-sanga, as many would gather at the temple this season, a very favorable time for such a visit. We went by way of Gyantze and were told that we would find a very fine chela who was known to all as "the laughing chela." His laughter and song carried him and his associates over many difficult places, healing many as he sang.

As we entered the courtyard of the Lamasery, a very fine upstanding fellow approached us with a hearty welcome, stating that they expected us to make the Lamasery our home during our stay in the village. We told him we were anxious to push on to the Phari Pass in the morning.

"Yes," he replied, "we understand that you are on your way to Pora-tat-sanga. I return there in the morning and shall be pleased to go with you if it is your wish."

We accepted and, with a hearty laugh, he conducted us to our quarters in the great hall of the

Lamasery. After making us comfortable, he bade us good night and took his departure, saying he would meet us in the early morning. As he walked away he sang in a well-modulated voice. This was the laughing chela. We were awakened in the morning at an early hour by his singing announcement that our morning meal was ready.

We bade the Lamas goodbye, received their blessing, and found all in readiness for our departure on the journey to Phari Pass. This led us past the mountain peaks of Phari and Kang La. In all, it was an arduous climb, but at the rough places the chela went ahead with laughter and song. At the more difficult places, his voice would ring out and it seemed as though it lifted us over them without an effort. We arrived at the top of the Pass at three o'clock in the afternoon.

To our surprise, instead of rugged mountains, we found a beautiful valley stretching out before us. This valley is called Chubi. Although it is sixteen thousand feet above sea level, either side of the valley is skirted by fine forests whose heavy leafy trees were very luxuriant. Ahead of us we saw villages with beautiful temples. We did not go through the valley but took the shorter trail by way of Tachi-cho-jong, then on to Pora-tat-sanga. Even this trail proved good. We had proceeded but a short distance, when we entered a beautiful forest with small streams on every hand. Here we saw an abundance of song birds and wild fowl. We had not encountered a predatory wild animal on the entire trip; this probably accounted for the abundance of wild life.

Our next stopping-place was at Maha Muni. Its fortress-like temple intrigued us; and here, as always, we received a hearty welcome. Those in charge told us that it would be useless to ask us to remain longer, as the Master Puriji had preceded us to the

Temple Pora-tat-sanga where many Yogis, Sadhus, and Gurus were gathering; and that we would have a goodly company on our last day's journey.

Early the next morning, the pilgrims were assembled, anxious to be on their way to keep their tryst with the great Master Puriji. All were eager to get the first glimpse of Pora-tat-sanga, — as they expressed it, a jewel set in a rock ledge, the most lofty of any temple in the world.

"Would we stay at Maha Muni when this great prize loomed just ahead of us?" sang the laughing chela. "Oh no. Fare thee well, Maha Muni, we love you and shall return to your tender embraces. To journey to Pora-tat-sanga is irresistible." So the cavalcade moved on. The great Everest was before us, standing out in the light of approaching dawn, stark and white in its robe of pure crystal. It seemed to beckon us to take just a few steps more, reach out our hands, and touch the hem of its garment. Yet when we had taken the few steps, its mass still eluded us. Chomolhari, its near neighbor, twenty-four thousand feet high, which we had passed, now seemed a pigmy compared with the monster just before us.

We thought the trail on its flanks stony and perilous but now we labored over a trail much of the distance on hands and knees. Still, the song and laughter of the chela bore us onward as though on wings.

In our enthusiasm, we forgot the dangers. It seemed that we accomplished these places instantly. The sun, while it dispelled the illusion of touching mighty Everest in another stride, revealed grandeurs of which description in words would only become a travesty. There were towers and great temples of nature crowned with crystal on every hand; but Everest, Great Everest, lay before us.

We saw it in the moonlight, with the first light of budding dawn, as the first rays of sunrise kissed its fair brow; then with the full rays of the noonday sun streaming down upon it; and again as the sun gradually faded and bade it goodnight, with the last rays bathing it in glory, the afterglow raising an answering glow toward heaven upon its great crest.

Can you, dear reader, not see why the trail that days was not long and arduous? It all passed in an instant. The vibrations of strength, peace, power, and harmony that are always sent forth from the temples but serve to urge travellers on to these peaks. Do you wonder that the Himalayas engender no fear in man? Do you wonder that poets never tire of singing their grandeur?

Finally, at nightfall the trails were all conquered and we stood gasping on a flat table-like rock of considerable extent.

In the distance before us were many temples but the jewel Pora-tat-sanga stood out two thousand feet above us, bathed in dazzling light. It seemed like a great arc lamp sitting in a crevice in the perpendicular rock wall; its light lighting up the rocks and temples all about us.

Here, in the amphitheater on the rock where we stood, was a great concourse of men and women. To our surprise we found that women were not barred from this pilgrimage; all who would, could come.

Here great Rishis have lived. Along this trail the Rishi Niri had passed. Thrice, the five brothers had passed over this trail, once alone, once with their great mother, and again with the great and good Darupati, the pride and grandeur of all womanhood. Here now sits Yogi Santi, the great, the pure, but the humble one in deep Samadhi.

"Where can all these great ones find shelter and food?" we suggested.

111

"Do not worry about food or shelter," sang the laughing chela. "There is an abundance here of food, shelter, and clothing for all."

"Sit down, every one," came in sweetest tones through the voice of the chela. No sooner were all seated than great bowls of nourishing hot food appeared. The Yogi Santi arose and began passing the food around, assisted by the chela and others. When their hunger was appeased, all arose and were conducted in groups to the neighboring temples, there to pass the night. The temple to which we were conducted by the chela was upon a perpendicular, table-like ledge, about seventy-five feet above where we and the others were standing. As we approached, we noticed a long pole with its base resting upon the rock where we stood, its top resting on the shelf-like rock above. As it seemed to be the only means of communication, we gathered at its base and looked up. As we stood thus, other groups joined us.

There were a number of other temples built in the niches formed by other ledges just above the first shelf. For a moment our only hope of shelter for the night seemed to depend upon our ability to negotiate this pole. Then the chela said, "Don't hurry." Through his voice came a great burst of song. "O loved one, through you we look for shelter this blessed night."

Instantly every one around stood silent for a moment. As with one voice, they spoke forth these words with dynamic power, "Such is the God power, A-U-M"; instantly all were standing on the rock ledge and we, with the rest, proceeded to our respective temples. When we arrived at the temples assigned to us, every trace of fatigue had left. We slept like babes that night. The emanations of power sent out by that group would have leveled mountains had it been so directed.

CHAPTER XII

THE next morning at four we were awakened by the voice of the chela, ringing out loud and clear, "Nature is waking; so should the children of nature awake. The morn of a new day is just dawning. The freedom of the day awaits you. A-U-M."

We went to the ledge where the top of the pole had rested the evening before and found to our surprise that the pole had been replaced by a well-built stairway. As we walked down, we wondered if we had been dreaming the night before.

The chela met us at the foot of the stairway and said, "No, you have not been dreaming. The stairs were dreamed there last night. The Master Puriji placed them there for the convenience of all; so you see they are a dream which came true."

During our stay of two weeks in that region, we were served with hot nourishing food. In no instance did we see food being prepared, yet we were bountifully served.

The chela and one other started to climb to the Pora-tat-sanga. The first approach was by means of crude steps cut in the rocks; then there were planks across fissures which made yawning canyons below. Part of the ascent was accomplished with the aid of ropes made fast in crevasses above. Although the two men climbed for two hours they made no headway beyond the second ledge which was about five hundred feet from their starting point. They decided they would be obliged to give it up.

When they hesitated, Yogi Santi, knowing their plight, called to them: "Why don't you come down?"

The chela replied, "We are making the attempt, but the rocks are holding us fast." They were having the experience of many, that it is easier to climb a sheer rock wall than to come down.

"Well, why not stay there?" jested the Yogi. "We will return tomorrow with food; perhaps by then you can climb to the top."

He then admonished them to keep perfectly calm, as he realized the difficult situation they were in. After three hours of careful direction they were with us again. With a sigh the Yogi murmured, "Thus wanes the enthusiasm of youth."

The youths looked longingly upward, "If Master Puriji stays there, it will probably be our bad luck to stay here. That trail is too troublesome for us."

"Don't worry," said the Yogi, "A higher one than yourself will take care of that. Now rest. You made an excellent start."

Many asked when we would be able to see the Great Master. The Yogi answered, "This evening." We wondered how a temple could have been built in the position Pora-tat-sanga occupied.

The Master Puriji came and talked with us during the evening meal. The failure of the attempt to climb to the temple was mentioned. The Master said that they had succeeded because they had made the second attempt.

At four the next evening, we all gathered below the temple. The Yogi Santi sat in Samadhi. Three of the company walked to a large flat stone and seated themselves as though in prayer. In a very few moments, the stone began to rise and all were carried to the temple on the stone.

Then Yogi Santi said to the chela and two others, "Are you ready?" "Yes," they all answered eagerly and sat down on the rock beside him. Instantly the rock began to move gently and together they were transported to the temple roof. Then our turn came. We were asked to stand in a group; then all arose to their feet and those at the temple came forward on the roof and began to chant A-U-M. In less time than it takes to relate, we were standing on the roof of the temple. Within the space of a few moments, all were gathered at the highest temple in the world.

When we were seated, the Master Puriji began speaking: "There are a number among you who have never witnessed body levitation and they wonder. Let me say there is no wonder about it, it is a power which belongs to man. We look upon it as knowledge of ancient Yoga. Many people have used it in the past and it was not looked upon as miraculous. Gautama Buddha visited many distant places through the levitation of his physical body. Thousands of people have I seen that have made the accomplishment and there are much greater evidences of power than this that you will see, evidences of a great irresistible force that can be used to move mountains when brought under complete control.

"You praise and sing of liberty and freedom from bondage and fear but, unless you have forgotten bondage and forgiven it, you have remembered bondage too well and have forgotten liberty. A system of pure Yoga is a message of complete freedom to the whole world.

"Let me give you an explanation of the A-U-M. In English the brief form OM is used. The right use in Hindustani is A-U-M. Therefore, we will consider it in this light.

" 'A' is a guttural sound. As you pronounce it, you will note it starts in the throat.

"To pronounce 'U', the lips must be thrust forward.

" 'M' you will note, is formed by pressing the lips together, causing a resonant tone like the humming

115

of a bee. Thus you will see that the sacred word of AUM is basic, comprehensive, all-inclusive, infinite. Its universe includes all names and forms.

"We know that form is perishable, but the concrete or real, before form was expressed, that which is named Spirit, is imperishable; for this reason we denote that imperishable reality, A-U-M.

"The Sadhu instructs his students thus, 'Tattoo-manu-asi.'

"When the students realize, through deep meditation and absolute Truth, they reply only 'Su-ham.' The teacher says to the student, 'Thou are God,' and the students reply, 'That I am, su-ham.'

"Let us look closer into the statement and the answers which the student gives when he realizes his Godhead, 'su-ham.' It contains two consonants and three vowels; the two consonants s and h, the three vowels a, u, and m which is a medial syllabic.

"The consonants cannot be pronounced unless joined to vowels. Thus in the domain of sound, the consonants represent the perishable, the vowels the imperishable.

"Therefore s and h are relegated to the perishable. A-U-M remains, and form AUM the eternal.

"O inquirer after Truth, AUM is the great GOD. Wise men attain their objective sustained by AUM. He who contemplates 'A,' the first part of AUM, contemplates God in the wakeful phase. He who meditates upon 'U,' the second part of AUM, the intermediate phase, obtains glimpses of the interior world and is of Spirit. He who meditates upon 'M,' the third part of AUM, sees God as himself, becomes illumined and is free immediately. Meditation upon AUM, the highest self, includes ALL.

"I am looking far out into the great white cosmos of light. There stands one with a simple gown of purest light drawn closely around him, the benevolence of pure light beaming from his countenance. From all around him comes the voice and through that voice the words 'You are forever and forever.' He comes nearer and nearer. The voice again speaks, 'This day and hour are given unto you, the priesthood of all human kind, that has no beginning and no end!' It is the focal point of the emanations of pure light, brought together to show all humanity their origin in Divinity. This is not the symbol of an order or brotherhood; it is the symbol of humanity in its pristine purity before a brotherhood began. The pristine condition has not yet spoken; this is long before the earth moved in its great nebula, long before this earth claimed its orbit and attracted that which belonged to it.

"This is the projection of the first human form that must stand forth in complete command of all force that starts to bind the atoms of the earth's nebula into form. Listen. The voice around him is speaking. The command is 'Let there be Light.' The dazzling white rays shoot forth, the form brings them to a focal point, the earth's nebula is bursting forth, and that focal point is the central sun of the nebula. As the central nucleus draws its atoms together, they take on more light. There is conscious direction back of this form that projects light rays to the focal point.

"Now the form is speaking and we hear the words. They are formed by letters of pure gold light; I can read them. 'I come from the great cosmos of light to watch you, O earth. Draw your particles to you. Into every particle project light which is eternal life, Light which is of the great Principle of Life, the Father, the emanations of all Life; and I declare unto you I AM.'

"Now I see the form beckoning. Standing with it are other forms and, from the midst, one speaks, 'Who is the dearly beloved that stands forth from the

Father, the light cosmos?' The voice from around again speaks in low whispered words, 'This is myself brought into form to have dominion, as I have dominion, and through myself my dominion manifests.' Lo, it is the Krishna, the Christos, the Christ, all three in ONE.

"The form again speaks and answers, 'I AM, and all of you are THAT I AM.' The voice continues, 'Look beyond me; the voice of God speaks through me. I AM God and you are God. Every soul in its pristine purity is God. The silent watchers sitting, hear the voice speaking through that form, saying, 'Behold, man is God, Again, the Christ of God comes from out the great Cosmos.'

"This is not emotion nor infatuation; this is a clear, calm vision of man, standing forth from God, in full dominion and mastership. This is the mastership of all humanity; not any one is excluded. Back of the form is pure crystal, dazzling white light emanations. It has come forth from pure white light, it is formed of pure white light; therefore, man is PURE WHITE LIGHT. Pure white light is God Life. Through man only do the pure rays of God Life emanate or manifest. As we fix and focalize our ideal through contemplation, the vision takes life, stands forth, comes closer and closer, until our vision and the form are united and stand forth as ourselves, and become one with us; then we become 'THAT.' Thus we say to all mankind, 'I AM YOURSELF expressing God.' When the true mother sees this at the time of conception, the immaculate conception takes place; then there is no rebirth. This is womanhood, manhood; wo-man-hood is God—the true Godhead of all humanity. This is Atma, the inclusion of soul in man and woman.

"Woman's true dominion is coexistent, coordinate with the image. The One is the ideal male and female. Together they are Darupati, the pride of motherhood, the ideal of womanhood, the eternal of humanity brought forth as helper and helpmate; many times destined to stand alone in perspective, but together in the whole of the Cosmos plan. In woman's true dominion, she offers her body on the altar of birth to be used to nurture and present the Christ child to the world. This is the true conception of the immaculate and, when presented in true thought, word, and deed, the child is not conceived in sin and born into iniquity but is pure, sacred, and holy, conceived of God, born of God, the image or Christ of God. Such a child need never go through rebirth. It is only through thoughts of the physical that the child is born into the physical and thereby allowed to assume the physical thoughts of sin and discord of the elders or parents. This alone makes rebirth necessary.

"When woman allows the Christ to stand forth from within, she is not only the Christ but the child is the Christ and is like Jesus. She then sees the Christ of God face to face.

"When wo-man, that which has wedded or brought together the male and female, sends forth her true call, her immaculate body is ready for that immaculate thing—the conception of the Christ Child—to be presented to the world. This body was prepared and projected forth for woman long before the world was projected into form."

Master Puriji ceased speaking. He invited us to accompany him to a great cave where sat many Yogis in Samadhi.

We lived at the temple and in this cave for nine days. Many of the Yogis have lived here for years and, when they come out of this seclusion, they do wonderful work among their people.

We were told that, after the assembly was over, a

number would be returning to India by way of Lake Sansrawar and Muktinath. Then from Muktinath we would go to Darjeeling very comfortably.

This was good news and we were greatly elated at the prospect of traveling with these great ones.

We went from cave to cave and talked to many of the Yogis and Sadhus; and, to our surprise, found that many of them were there summer and winter. When asked if they were troubled with snow, they replied that no snow fell in the vicinity and that there were no storms or fogs.

Time passed on swift wings and the eve of our departure was upon us.

CHAPTER XIII

T HE morning of our departure, the community was awakened at three o'clock by the voice of the chela chanting. We were aware that something unusual was happening, as he was inviting all to come forth for a moment.

As we stepped out from the temple, the light from Pora-tat-sanga blazed forth so brightly that the whole section was aglow. The chela stood on the corner of the temple and asked for silent contemplation. We could see hundreds of forms standing with their arms upraised.

The silence was broken by the words, "Hail, Hail, Hail, the Master Puriji chants." Thousands of voices joined in. The echo gave the effect of many more thousands. In the stillness of the morning, every word could be heard.

These were his words: "Could there be a God of the Hindu, a God of the Mongol, a God of the Jew, and a God of the Christian? There is a true Universal Principle, Director, Primal, Infinite and Divine. The central light of that principle is called God. God must enfold all. God does enfold all. All are God. This surely does not mean a God of just one and not for all.

"When we speak of God, we speak of one and all, for all, in all, through all, and of all. Should the Hindu name his God and say there is no other, his thought is divided. Should the Mongol name his God and say there is no other, his thought is divided. Should the Jew name his God and say there is no other, his thought is divided. Should the Christian name his God and say there is no other, his thought is divided. A house divided unto itself is shattered and must fall. United it does maintain forever. Choose you whom you will serve. Division is failure and death. Unity in the Father-Mother Principle is eternal progress, honor, and dominion. A-U-M. A-U-M. A-U-M."

It seemed as though this AUM reverberated around the whole world. We could hear the echoes of the AUM-reverberations for at least ten minutes, as though a temple gong had sounded. At times it seemed as though the rocks themselves were giving forth the AUM. As these reverberations gradually ceased, all gathered in the great rock amphitheater below us and we joined the assembly.

When we were seated with our group, Yogi Santi raised his arms above his head and, in unison, all chanted the AUM as before. Again the rocks seemed to send forth the vibrations. This lasted till the meal was finished.

As we arose, all stood silent for a moment. Then sang the chela: "We shall bid you farewell; and our greatest blessing we leave, as we depart from your most gracious presence. May we ask the honor of a return welcome?

"We hesitate to depart and know that we with longing hearts and eyes shall look forward to our return. We bid you farewell. May the richest blessings of all that is holy be bestowed upon you."

The reply came as though with one voice: "Loved ones, we are never parted, though you may think space separates us. Not so; distance has no power to separate, for God and yourself permeate all space. We need not even say farewell, for we see you at all times, face to face. You do not go, you do not come, you are always here. There is no time, no parting, no passing; the present is here, hence the future also. Where can we be except we are all together in God?

Do not go hence but come hither and you are always here."

As the last words floated out to us, we were well on the trail. While our steps were retreating, we were still there. There was no parting and we have never felt that we actually left that sacred place.

All day long the chela laughed and sang. Again his laughter and song lifted us bodily, as it were, over the most difficult places.

We arrived again at Maha Muni, the silent one, at two o'clock that afternoon. Instead of stopping for the night, we pushed on and, though we travelled for sixteen hours and covered over seventy miles that day, we were not fatigued. Thus we travelled to Sansrawar. Here we were conducted to a beautiful temple near the lake, where we rested for two days before pushing on through the Trans-Himalaya Pass. This is a near-Paradise. The lake rests like a jewel in a great mountain setting. Birds sang from the trees all about.

Here, the greater portion of the party lived. We would go on to Muktinath with Yogi Santi, the laughing chela accompanying our party. We had often heard of the difficulties of this pass but, although we were many days on the trail, we encountered very few difficulties and reached Muktinath in due time. There we were again greeted by Emil and a number of our friends.

No words can convey the pleasure we experienced at this reunion. We had travelled far and had been accorded the greatest hospitality and kindness; yet here we experienced the thrill of a true homecoming.

While we were relating some of our experiences that evening, Emil said: "Now you know why the Tibetans, at altitudes of twenty-one thousand feet, are apparently undisturbed with heavy loads upon their backs. Now you know how they climb Mount

Everest as they claim. They go to the crest of the God of Mountains, as they call Mount Everest. They overcome, or come up over, the god of the mountain just as they overcome the god of any burden. In other words, they let go the burden; then the burden does not exist. You cannot put a burden upon the shoulders, much less upon the form, of the true God-man. Now you may see the truth in Jesus' statement, 'Come unto me, all ye that are weary and heavy laden and I will give you rest.' The true statement was, 'I AM does give you rest.' When you rest in the I AM, you change from the god of burden, to GOD that is rest and peace. You have come up over the god of burden to the Father of rest; therein you carry no burdens. God the Father is man's power to think rightly and directly through any condition.

"Man, as the poor worm of the dust, is not in God consciousness; this is man expressing in the worm consciousness, only.

"If you are shooting at a target and you wish to hit the mark, you must focus your whole thought upon the center of the target; then, with your will in complete focus, you must see nothing but the mark. When you have hit the mark, you have brought forth or accomplished God in a degree.

"God is your divine ideal, the focal point upon which every thought and act is centered. It is in this way that you bring forth the divine spiritual man, the Christ of God, the word made flesh. The flesh is God, as well as God is around the flesh. Make your subjective one objective, a willing and all-wise worker with God, Principle. Head straight for your objective; make that objective the divine spiritual life that God within you is, and God sees for all. No one ever accomplished anything unless, with all his will in complete focus, he held his objective (God) directly before the pure mirror of his thought force. That thought force is himself acting as God, demanding of himself that his attention be so thoroughly focused upon his objective (God), that it (God) is brought forth instantly. The instant God is objectified, present the mould or pattern you desire and it is filled full. If this were not an absolute fact, you would not, nor could you, have thought of your desire. When your desire is set forth in this way, it is divine. With your divinity always projected, your desire is conceived in divine order. It is wholly within your power to say when it shall come forth. You are always in command. You have all power to speak the word of authority. To all outer things your command is 'complete silence.' Now you can say definitely and knowingly, 'There is no greater power than the Christ within me. I now send forth my Christ-endowed word; it does accomplish all things instantly. There is no greater driving force than my Christ-endowed word. I praise, bless, and send it forth with abundance, harmony, and perfection.' You have first spoken the word (God) which represents your true desire. Never go back again to the asking (this attitude engenders doubt); but go on, recall what you have done. You have put forth your Christ word; you are in command. The thing is finished and complete; it is in divine order.

'I thank you, God, for Life and Light
Abundant, full and free;
For perfect, boundless, wealth and power,
Unhampered liberty.'

Recall that if any two unite their spiritual force, they can conquer the world, even though singly they can do nothing. These *two* are *God* and *you*, united in one purpose. If others will unite with you with the same sincerity of purpose, your power becomes greater as the square of the number of persons. Thus, every person standing forth one with God and united with you becomes the power that is increasing fourfold.

"If two of you shall unite with God as touching any one thing they shall ask, it is done for them of my Father. My God becomes your God and we are together. Together with God, man conquers that which is not Godlike.

"Go into your closet (your God-self), shut the door to all else, close the outer eyes, see singly your true God-self. You have quietly put yourself into a spiritually receptive mood.

"God Principle is the one point. I am one with Universal Life Energy. It is flowing through me now. I know it, I feel it. I thank God my Father that I have the ability to accomplish all things.

"When you pray to God, with I AM in direct contact with all Universal Life Energy, you are using it in limitless measure. God is the name you give to the all-wise, intelligent Spirit, and this spirit is within as well as without every human being. It is necessary for you to let God stand forth through you into outer expression. Therefore, it is not necessary to seek knowledge and help from outside sources, when you know that the source of all knowledge, the spirit of all knowledge, the understanding truth is latent within you. Why seek knowledge from without, as God the Universal Spirit is within? Through this understanding, you call upon this principle when you accomplish any one thing, you know that the God within is the greatest of teachers.

"You realize that all the power you possess is first drawn to you, then generated within your body and sent forth to accomplish whatever you direct it to bring forth. This is God emanating through you; not a personal god, but an all-inclusive God within you.

126

When you let God stand forth from within, you are connected with God, as God interpenetrates all conditions. By worshipping God within and seeing God standing forth from you, you are worshipping God, the Deity in the whole human family. To worship an outside deity is to bring forth idolatry. To worship God within and to see God standing forth, from within out to all the world, is to bring forth and be in conscious contact with the emanations of God life and light everywhere.

"There cannot be a deity outside of your body that is not within your body, as all is vibrating or emanating energy. Thus, these vibrations flow through your body as well as around it and the vibrations of Deity include every atom of your whole body as well as the whole mass of the Universe. Thus, you put God everywhere, before all, within all, around all, enveloping all, and enfolding all. There is not an atom of space that does not have the emanating energy of light and life flowing through it."

Having finished this discourse, Emil stated that they would meet us in Hardwar and bade us good night.

127

CHAPTER XIV

A S we neared Hardwar, about a day's journey
from the city, we stopped at the home of an
American whom we called Weldon. He gave us
a hearty welcome and insisted upon our remaining
with him for a few days.

Weldon, a well-known writer, who had lived in
India for many years, was in sympathy with and
deeply interested in our work. He had asked several
times to join our party, but circumstances had been
such that we could not include him. As we sat in his
garden next day, relating our experiences, Weldon
suddenly remarked that he had never fully accepted
the authenticity of the history and life of the man
called Jesus of Nazareth. He had studied available
records carefully but they had all seemed vague and
lacking in conclusion. Finally, he had given up in
despair, as there were very grave doubts in his mind
that such a character existed. Our Chief asked him if
he were brought face to face with this man, did he
think he would know Him, and how would he recognize Him?

Weldon replied: "You have touched upon a subject that has been the greatest motivating ideal of my
whole life. You will never know the absorbing interest with which I have looked forward to some sign of
actual truth of the man's existence in bodily form
upon this earth. Each year my doubts have grown
stronger until I have despaired of ever finding a
trace that I can place full confidence in. However,
there has always been something away back somewhere that I might define as a vague thought or ray
of hope that sometime, somewhere, if I could meet

this man face to face without a suggestion from any outside source, I would know Him positively. Instinctively this thing wells up before me; and I say this to you, — I have never before voiced it, — I know I would know Him. This is the most sincere feeling I have ever experienced and, if you will pardon me for the repetition, I will say again, I know I would know Him."

That evening as we were preparing to retire, our Chief came to us and said: "You all heard the conversation regarding the man Jesus this afternoon. You recognized the sincerity of our friend. Shall we invite him to go with us? We do not know nor have we any way of determining whether this man that is known as Jesus of Nazareth will be at our destination. We cannot check his movements; in fact, we only know that he has been there. If we invite Weldon to go and the man is not there, will it not result in further disappointment and serve no good purpose? Weldon seems anxious to go with us; since none of us knows that this man Jesus will be there, there will be no suggestion from any of us in any way. In this, I think the time is auspicious." We all agreed.

The next morning our Chief invited Weldon to accompany us. Instantly his face lighted up with anticipation. After a moment's reflection, he said he had an assignment for the following Wednesday and would be obliged to return by that time. As this was Thursday, he would have six days. Our Chief thought the time sufficient; so we decided to leave that afternoon. We went well and we reached our destination before noon of the second day.

As we arrived, we noticed a group of twelve people sitting together in the garden of the lodge we were to occupy. As we approached they all arose and the owner of the lodge came forward to greet us. In the group we saw the man Jesus standing. Before anyone could say a word or make a suggestion, Weldon had stepped from our midst, with both hands extended; and with a joyous exclamation rushed forward, clasping Jesus' hands in his, saying, "O, I knew you, I knew you. This is the most divine moment of my whole life."

When we realized what had taken place, there was something akin to divine joy that swept through us as we beheld the rapture of our friend. We stepped forward and exchanged greetings as Weldon was introduced to the group.

After lunch, while sitting in the garden, Weldon said to Jesus, "Won't you talk to us? I have been waiting a lifetime for this moment."

There was silence for a few moments, then Jesus began: "In the silence of the hour, I would have you know that the Father to whom I speak and who dwells within me, is the same loving Father who dwells in all and to whom all can speak and know just as intimately as I do.

"A breath of wondrous glory sweeps across the chords that vibrate with a life pure and divine. It is so pure that the waiting silence stops, and intently listens; the fingers of the great and knowing One of yourself, touches your hand with lingering softness; and the voice as always is telling you of the Father's great and glorious love. Your voice is saying to you, 'I know you are with me, and together you and I are God.' Now the Christ of God stands forth. Won't you erase every limitation and stand with me in spirit? Greater thoughts have not been given than these I give unto you. It does not matter that men say it cannot be. You, each one of you, are standing forth the Divine Master, conquering and in full dominion, just as you have seen me conquer. The time is here; the fulfilling pure thought that you have sent out to the Divine Master has come to fruition in your own body and the soul has taken complete command. With me you soar to heights celestial.

"We lift these bodies up until their shining radiance becomes a blaze of pure, white light and together we have returned to the Father from whence all have come forth.

"God our Father is pure light emanation and from this vibrating light all come forth; in this vibration all stand together with God. In these vibrating emanations of light all material consciousness is erased and we see creations projected forth from the formless into form, all things renewed every instant. In the primal cosmos, aqueous or God substance, all things exist and, because of that existence, the vibrations are so high that none perceive them. Unless one stands forth in spirit as we do, it is necessary to raise the vibrations of the body to spirit vibrations.

"Now we can see creation going on all the time, as creation is caused by the radiation of cosmic light vibrations generated in the great Cosmos; and this radiation is the great universal life or light energy that sustains all and is called the Father of radiation or vibration. It is the Father of radiation because its radiation will shatter any other radiation or vibration. In reality it only sets them aside in order that other forms may take their place.

"When our body vibrates in tune with Spirit vibrations, we are light vibrations, the greatest of all vibrations, God the Father of all vibrations.

"It will soon be proved that these cosmic rays constitute such a terrific bombardment that they are destructive to so-called matter. These rays are from the source of all energy, the Father of all elements, the source from which all elements come. This is not destruction, this is transmutation from so-called matter to spirit form.

131

"It will soon be known that these cosmic rays have such tremendous penetrating power that they penetrate through all mass, shattering as it were, the very heart or nucleus of a so-called atom, transmuting it into atoms of other substance and thereby creating other elements of higher order; and in this way, creation advances into a higher emanation of pure light or life itself.

"These radiations, which have such tremendous penetrating power, are readily distinguished from all radiations coming from the earth or sun galaxy and have complete control over all these radiations or vibrations. It will soon be known that these radiations come from a universal source, unseen, and that the earth is continuously subjected to a terrific bombardment of these rays that are so potent they change or transmute atoms of one element into the Infinite particles of another element. It will also be found that when this cosmic ray strikes the nucleus of an atom, it does shatter it. It separates this atom into the minute particles of another substance, causing transmutation from a lower to a higher element. Thus, these radiations do not destroy matter; they transmute it from a lower to a higher element, — from the material to spiritual.

"This higher element is as man dictates; it is higher as he names and uses it for a higher purpose. When man stands forth in spiritual vibrations, he can fully determine and regulate these rays and their mode of action.

"Thus to man, standing in spiritual vibrations, transmutation is going on all the time all about him. Transmutation is but creation in the higher sense. Thus all are created where they stand. Creation never ceases; it is continuous, never ending.

"The emanations of radiation from the Cosmos are made up of light and are composed of so-called

132

light bullets that burst forth from the Cosmos. This greater Universe is around and encloses and surrounds all universes, to the extent that the suns absorb and bring into its central sun, conserve, concentrate and build up, all the energy that is dissipated from the universes. This central sun becomes so full of vibrating, pulsing energy, and this energy becomes so condensed that the so-called light bullets are shot out with such radiating force that, when they collide with the nucleus of another atom, that atom is shattered but not destroyed. Its particles are transmuted into particles of other elements which are finally assimilated into the element to which they belong; then that element comes to life.

"Life is the energy that is released by this so-called bombardment of light bullets; and that portion absorbed by the particles released is called the life of the particle, or of the whole element; while the portion of the energy released but not absorbed as life, is returned or drawn back to the Cosmos as it were. It is again concentrated and condensed until it can be again shot forth to collide with and shatter other atoms, thus creating the particles that go to create the atom of another element.

"Thus creation is continuous, everlasting; expanding and concentrating, then through reduced vibrations, condensing into form.

"This intelligent, emanating, Energy—is God, controlling the universe around us, as well as controlling the universe of our bodies which are spiritual and not material.

"This transmutation is not disintegration. The intelligence so directs that only a few of these light bullets strike the nuclei of other atoms, at a time ratio and in complete conformity to law, so that no manifestation is overbalanced.

"Man, one with this supreme intelligence, can in

an orderly way, step up this impingement, so that his needs are fulfilled instantly. In this way, man hastens the slow process of nature. He does not interfere with nature; he works with nature in a higher rate of vibration than that in which nature works in the lower order of concept. 'Lift up your eyes and look on the fields; for they are white already to harvest.' [St. John 4:35]. All is vibration and corresponds to the plane or field upon which vibration acts. The planes or fields spoken of have no reference to the concentric bands or shells that surround the earth. These concentric shells or layers are ionization bands which enclose the earth and reflect back vibrations originating on the earth but they do not impede or shut out Cosmic light rays. It is through them that transmutation or creation is going on all the time. Even our bodies are transmuted from a lower to a higher condition and we become the conscious directors of this change by keeping the thoughts and, therefore, the body attuned consciously to the higher vibrations. Thus we attune the body consciously to a higher vibratory rate and we become that vibration.

"In this condition the master waits. As you stand now, you are master, you are ruler over all conditions. Now you know that the glory and the consciousness of a Divine creation is far above any material thought.

"The first step is fully and completely to control all outer activities of thought, mind, and body, with the thought always uppermost that you are cultivating the habit of perfection, the God habit, the Christ-of-God habit. Do this wherever you are, every time it comes to you during your working or resting hours. See this perfect presence within you. Get into the habit of seeing this perfect presence as your real self, this Christ-of-God presence. Then go a little further. See a Divine White Light, dazzling in purity and brilliance emanating forth from the very center of your being. See it shining forth with such brilliance and glory that it emanates from every cell, fibre, tissue, muscle, and organ of your whole body. Now see the true Christ of God standing forth, triumphant, pure, perfect, and eternal. Not the Christ of *me,* but your own true Christ of God, the only begotten of your Father God, the only true son of God, the triumphant and all conquering Godhead. Step forth and claim this as your divine right and it is yours.

"Every time you say, 'God,' know fully that you are presenting God; and you will do the world a greater service by so doing than by presenting me as the Christ of God. It is far greater and nobler to see yourself as the Christ of God, you yourself presenting God to the world and beholding God as yourself.

"You sit back and pray to me to intercede for you. It is wonderful that you do present me to the world as the Christ of God and recognize the God qualities presented through me, just so long as you do not make an idol or image of me and then pray to that idol. The moment you make a graven image of me and pray to that image, you debauch me and yourselves. It is well to see the ideal that I or anyone else presents, then make that ideal your very own. Then we are not apart or separate from God; as such, man conquers the world. Do you not see the greater thing to be accomplished by standing forth ONE with us in God?

"If you cultivate this with love, reverence, devotion, and worship, it becomes a habit and soon it is all of you, your daily life and existence. In a short time you have brought forth Divinity. You are once more the Divine Christ, the first-born of God. You are One with Primal Spirit, Energy. Actually feel, see, and take hold of this Great Light; accept, declare, and know positively that it is yours; and in a short time, your body will actually send forth this light.

"In every age and every condition, all through the great immensity, this supreme light has existed; it is everywhere. This light is life.

"When anything is made plain, we are enlightened regarding it. The light shines forth into our conscious concept. Soon the LIGHT of LIFE will shine forth to your watching eye, as it has to all great ones. Many of these great ones are portrayed standing forth in a great blaze of light. Although you may not see it, this light is real and is life, radiating from your body."

Here Weldon asked if we might talk over some of the Bible teachings; and Jesus readily assented. We arose and walked out of the garden together. Weldon exclaimed, "Just think! Here you have contacted these people and I have lived in the same neighborhood and never recognized them. This day has indeed been a revelation to me. A new world, a new light, a new life stands revealed."

We asked him how he recognized the man Jesus. He answered, "You marvel that I recognized the man for what he is. I do not know how I know. I know and nothing can shake that knowing."

We suggested that if he kept his assignment, it would be necessary for him to leave the following Monday and that two of our party would leave for Darjeeling on that day and would accompany him.

"Leave," he replied. "I have already dispatched a messenger asking another person to take my assignment. I am staying here. You just try to send me away."

CHAPTER XV

A FTER a most interesting day going about the countryside, visiting many places of interest, we returned to the lodge at eight o'clock and found our friends assembled in the garden.

After a short talk on general subjects, Jesus spoke, saying they realized that Weldon was mystified. He went on to say: "I shall talk to you just as I wish you to talk to yourself. If you will make these statements true or make them a part of yourself, you will need no other. These statements are in no wise to be used as formulas. Students can use them to bring their thoughts in accord with Divine Principle or, as many say, 'to train their thoughts to the one point.' We use the word GOD as often as possible, repeating it many times.

"It is a well known fact that the oftener you say or use the word GOD, knowing it to be the highest principle in-dwelling and flowing through you, the greater benefit you will derive from it. Allow me to repeat, —our thought is, 'You cannot say GOD or use the name too much.'

"See God as Creative Principle flowing through you; concentrate and energize that principle, and send it out with more dynamic influence. Because of the fact that it always flows through you as well as around you, you are able to give it a greater impetus by sending it out with the whole force of your being, impelling it outward. Man's body is the medium through which this force is transformed and added impetus is given it, in order to do a greater work and be sent forth in greater form.

"Thus, there is far greater force added to this

137

principle through the fact that millions are magnifying its radiations and sending them out; yet one man standing forth in full dominion can conquer the world. Thus, you see what millions could accomplish.

"The more you use this name, knowing that it is the in-dwelling God Principle that you are establishing within you, the higher the rate of vibration of your body. These vibrations become correlated and respond to the Divine vibrations which the word God means and gives forth. Should you say GOD once, meaningly, your body will never return to the same vibratory rate that it was giving off at the time you used the word GOD. With this thought in mind, make these statements your very own; put them in your own language if you so desire. They are from you and not from any outside source. Just try for a time and see what it will do for you. Recall that every time you think GOD, you are God's Divine Plan. These are not my words, they are your words coming from the Christ of God, yourself. Bear in mind that Jesus, the man, became the Christ as He expressed light, which is pure life or God.

"God, my Father, the Divine Principle flowing through me, is all; and all that God is, I AM. I am the Christ of God, God-man.

"All that God my Father is, is for God-man to use; thus I AM is entitled to use all substance. In fact, God my Father is pressing out all substance to God-man in unlimited measure.

"God Principle is my Father; I AM the Christ of God; both in whole and complete union. All that God has, the Christ of God is.

"Let us take the word GOD. Why is it that this word has so much power? It is because of the vibrations that are released when the word is spoken — they are of the very highest, they are the Cosmos, the most effective vibration. They come in on the Cosmic Ray and set up the highest field of radiation. This field is all-inclusive, all-penetrating, all-existing, and rules all mass. They are the ruling elements of all energy and this vibration is the vehicle that carries light and life.

"The ruling intelligence back of this radiation is what we term GOD and, through its radiation, the intelligence pervades everything. From this radiation field both light and life emanate. When man accepts these, he unites them in his body; they are one. This body responds immediately to the light vibration and he is God vibration; his body radiates light. Thus, one standing forth as God is often invisible to one functioning in a lower vibratory field. This is the reason that the word GOD is so powerful.

"Because of this sustaining word GOD, your Bible has maintained such influence and longevity. Think of the number of times the word is written and thus, spoken, in that great book. See the different lines of radiation of light and therefore, life and energy that go out from each word either written or spoken. Each word carries its vibrations to the very soul of all who speak, hear, or see the word GOD; and as the soul responds to that vibration, the book from which the radiations come forth is lifted and exalted correspondingly as the soul is exalted by the vibrations. Thus, the book is given life, power, and immortality. It is in reality the word GOD that has accomplished this. Thus, you can say that the book is the word of God in the spiritual sense and not in the literal sense of the word.

"Too many take the Bible literally, instead of giving attention to its true spiritual value. This lack of consciousness matters little, as the spiritual vibrations set aside those set up by this attitude of thought. When they think or say GOD once, those vibrations far outweigh their lack of understanding.

"It is the survival of the Bible that has proved such a stumbling-block to the scoffer and critic. The atheist fails utterly to explain why the word GOD supersedes and has complete dominion over the word Evil.

"Repeat God thoughtfully for a time, then try to set up a vibration in your body with the word Evil. If you have not already experienced this, it will be a revelation to you. Many scientists proclaim that the theistic hypothesis is impossible. Do not mind them, for the things which they pronounced impossible yesterday are being accomplished today.

"Do you not know that it is high time to go within your house, put it in order, and find out what the Word GOD will do for you? Think attentively for a moment, try it and see if it will not cause you to drop all differences and bickerings. Speak GOD with your whole soul and feel the exhilaration that causes you to treat your brother more kindly and deal with him more justly. Place God before you and the mist of the long-forgotten ages will be dispelled as a wisp of smoke. The intellect may frown upon this. Don't mind the intellect; it has erred many times. Stand forth with the word GOD dominant within you and a whole world of strife and confusion cannot touch you.

"When you know positively that GOD or supreme vibration does exist and that it is ALL POWER, you can use it to accomplish ALL THINGS. With it you can transport yourself from place to place. If you are in one place and the need is for you to be elsewhere, recall it is the self that is holding you stationary, not GOD. You are using God power in limitation if you remain where you are. Let go of self, erase limitation, put forth the command that you are the Christ of God, one with the God vibration and power. The instant you make it definite that you are God vibration, you will be at your destination. Just thinking a thing does not accomplish that thing. YOU MUST KNOW AND DO; then love and worship the source or principle enough to do it.

"Faith shows the way through thought; but it takes the actual command of the Christ of God, that you are that vibration. The instant you allow that vibration to take full command, you GET UP AND DO IT. The KNOWING through love and worship becomes the accomplishment. That you are unconscious of their radiations does not set aside the fact of their existence. Through faith in their existence, then knowing that they do exist, you become conscious of their existence; then you can use them.

"When you express a vibration and are in tune with that vibratory field, you are invisible to things that express in a lower vibratory field. Thus, if your body vibrates with the speed of light, you are invisible to those that cannot see light. Light is Life; thus, if you live wholly in the vibrations of light, your body is pure life. Light, and Life, is God. Thus all are GOD when they live in the God vibration.

"'The sun shall be no more thy light by day; neither for brightness shall the moon give light unto thee; but the Lord shall be unto thee an everlasting light and thy God, thy glory.' [Isa. 60:19.] The Lord Christ of God has no more need of light when his body vibrations are in unison with God vibrations. His body is light, purer than that of the noonday sun. The Lord (or law of) God, expressing pure life (light) through Jesus or man, becomes the Christ upon earth. Each man becomes the Christ when the Lord (law) or law of God is understood and actually lived.

141

" 'I AM the light of the world: he that followeth me shall not walk in darkness but shall have the light of life.'

" 'The Pharisees therefore said unto him, Thou bearest record of thyself; thy record is not true. Jesus answered and said unto them, Though I bear record of myself, yet my record is true: for I know whence I came and whither I go; but ye cannot tell whence I come, and whither I go. Ye judge after the flesh; I judge no man. And yet, if I judge, my judgment is true: for I am not alone but I and the Father that sent me. It is also written in your law that the testimony of two men is true. I am one that bears witness of myself and the Father that sent me beareth witness of me.

" 'Then said they unto him, Where is thy Father? Jesus answered, Ye neither know me, nor my Father: if ye had known me, ye should have known my Father also.' [8:12-19.]

"How can you walk in darkness if you walk hand in hand with God? If you let God triumph, your works and accomplishments are eternal. You came forth with this vibration and as long as you live true to this light, you will never perish or change — these vibrations go on forever.

"Many have lived noble lives and accomplished noble deeds, all accomplished through God vibrations. Thus they have the power to create by lowering these vibrations and allowing the aqueous substance to consolidate into form. Aqueous substance is that substance which contains all elements. Scientists will discover that all elements can be resolved into this aqueous or vaporous condition. In this state, all substance vibrates or radiates at the same rate of vibration. Thus, by lowering the vibrations to the rate at which the particles of the element will coalesce or come together, you may produce the element desired. Here the Cosmic radiations play an important part. Here the transmutation takes place.

"Many great souls have lived and their works have passed with them, because they were unconscious of the power that sustained them. They, as well as others, were unconscious of their works and thus were forgotten. Had they recognized this power and then, through definite thought and action consolidated these deeds, their accomplishments would have stood forth as a mountain that could not be forgotten; the same as the great mountains of accomplishments that stand forth before humanity today, as, for example, the Great Pyramid of Egypt.

"Is it not much greater to live the Christ life? Is it not worthwhile to make this your ideal? Does this not completely erase the petty things of life? Do you not see the accomplishments of the ones that dared to step forth and live the Christ Life?

"As you accomplish this, you stand on the Mount of Transfiguration.

"Man's law and prophecy disappear and the triumphant Christ stands alone, but not lonely. You can do this, all can do it, if they but will.

"Now you know that you and the Father are One. This is the testimony of two standing together as one law and this testimony IS TRUE. Thus, if you judge, your judgment is true. If you bear record of this origin, your record is true. As you know your origin with the Father, you never pass on, you always know the Father. 'If they had known one, that is my Father, they would have known me,' for our vibrations would have been in perfect accord.

"'Then cried Jesus in the temple as he taught, saying, Ye both know me, and ye know whence I am: and I am not come of myself, but he that sent me is true, whom ye know not. But I know him: for I am from him, and he hath sent me.

" 'Then they sought to take him: but no man laid hands on him, because his hour had not yet come. And many of the people believed in him and said, When Christ cometh, will he do more miracles than these which this man hath done?

" 'Then said Jesus unto them, Yet a little while am I with you, and then I go unto him that sent me. Ye shall seek me, and shall not find me: and where I am, thither ye cannot come.' [John 7:28-34.]

"You know that the spiritual and material is merged within the Christ. Spirit knows, 'I come not of myself, I am of the Father.' The temple (body) must become a pure channel through which the Christ shines forth. When the Christ is risen in the individual, then will he do greater miracles than these which I have done. As you seek, you will find the Christ in me and the Christ in you, brothers one and all.

"Your hour shall come when the Christ appears to each one of you as an individual; then will you be lifted up into the Christ consciousness and glorify the Father as I have glorified Him.

"It is written [in Matthew 27:46] that my last words on the cross were: 'My God, my God, why hast thou forsaken me?' This is a complete mistranslation. The words actually were: 'My God, my God, thou hast never forsaken me or any of thy children, for thy children can come to thee as I have come. They can see my life as I have lived my life. Thus, by living that life, they do incorporate the Christ and become One with you, God my Father.'

"There was never a thought of desertion or separation. The Christ of God stood forth definitely, long before that hour. Had they burned my body, I could have reassembled it from the same particles that were released in the seeming destruction. Had they divided every particle of the body, it could have been reassembled instantly; there would have been no change.

"Man is so constituted that when he stands forth with the understanding of the Christ of God, he releases enough intelligent energy and that energy and intelligence so completely envelop him that, should the body be disintegrated and the life element become separated from the particles, this intelligent life principle could reassemble and consolidate those same particles in the same form in which it had expressed itself. The mould or pattern is there; it is built of, and in, the substance which cannot be destroyed. It would only be necessary to reassemble the substance and fill the mould, interpenetrated with the same life element, and you would have the perfect pattern or image as before.

"Thus, you can see that the crucifixion did not harm me; it harmed only those who attempted to harm the Christ Principle. It was an example of the fulfilling law of the Great Principle, a pathway which all humanity may follow. Thus following, they become the Christ of God, their ideal consolidated into imperishable form. Not even this body was destroyed. Its vibrations were so high that the mere act of fastening it to and raising it upon the cross was but a symbol that those who crucified me had finished all limitation which the mortal could put upon the body. The necessity for the completion of the fulfillment of mortal limitation was to place the body in the tomb and roll a great stone thereon and completely seal the tomb. Thus the cry: 'It is finished.'

"When the mortal is finished, immortality is complete. Thus it is impossible to confine the immortal body of man even in a rock-hewn tomb. The rock could have been dissolved to release such a body, had such a necessity arisen. Thus you see that the whole scene was a symbol of man's heritage."

145

CHAPTER XVI

THESE gatherings continued for a number of days. It was decided that Gordon Weldon and I would stay with these people, while the chief and the others would return to Darjeeling where the party would establish headquarters, in order to assemble and tabulate the data which we had secured.

After they had departed we established our camp more permanently, as this would be our headquarters until our Chief returned in December.

Our location was at the crest of a ridge extending into the valley from a spur of the main mountain mass, at an elevation of about five hundred feet above the valley floor. The location and setting were most advantageous for a main camp, as it was readily accessible to many different places which we wished to visit.

The camp was in the midst of a great grove of tall, stately trees. The ground sloped gradually from the main ridge toward our camp, giving it the appearance of nestling in the center of a crescent-shaped amphitheatre, with the valley as a great mural enclosing the other segment. Beyond and over the mural, the sun went down in a sea of liquid gold. Every evening this color was reflected upon the upward-sloping surface of the ridge that served as the background of our amphitheatre, bathing the crest of the ridge in a sea of throbbing, pulsing color, like unto a gigantic halo.

As one stood in silence, just as the last rays of the sun were shut off by the horizon, one could imagine a great Being with arms outstretched at the level of the shoulders, a robe of pure gold draped in most artistic folds, drawn closely around, with an aura of pure white light blazing out for miles.

One evening, as we sat near our campfire just before sunset, the sun seemed to be blazing forth with the most magnificent brilliance; so evident was the unusual phenomenon that every member of our party was entranced. One remarked to a Sanyasi, who had arrived a few moments before, that the sun was attempting to outdo itself before bidding us good night. "An auspicious event portends," replied the Sanyasi. "A mella of great souls, accompanying a most high one, gathers here shortly. Quiet please."

Instantly a hush as though from outer space seemed to settle over the scene. Suddenly a heavenly voice burst through the stillness in most melodious and heavenly cadence. Then thousands of the Kokila chimed in with a thrilling high-pitched treble that blended with the voice and song so harmoniously that one could but believe that the cantata was heaven-born. Could you, dear reader, have witnessed the scene and heard the song, I know you would pardon the superlatives.

In a moment the treble of the birds was silent, but the song floated on more majestically than ever. Then, on the slope of the ridge, there appeared two angelic female figures, robed in shimmering silvery folds, which gave a dim outline of mystically beautiful forms. So beautiful were the features, that one can only say, "Why outrage them with mere words?"

We, as well as the Sanyasi, sat enthralled, forgetting to breathe for a moment. Suddenly thousands of voices joined in the chorus; then forms began to assemble and circle about the two central figures. The song ceased as suddenly as it began and the figures disappeared. Absolute silence reigned supreme and a great form appeared as before but in a greater array of brilliant color. As the sun's rays faded, the form gradually diminished until, standing before us was a well-shaped manly form, with a perfect, symmetrical figure and flowing hair of matchless color. His body was clad in a shimmering white robe, which fell from his shoulders in layer upon layer of artistic folds; clasped around the waist was a loose silver-white girdle, the hem of his robe just brushing the grass as he advanced toward us with stately strides. A Greek god could not have looked more majestic.

As he came close, he paused and said: "We do not need to be introduced; we need not be formal. I salute you as true brothers. I extend my hand and clasp that of myself. Do I hesitate to embrace myself? Not so, for I love you as myself. Together with God Principle, we love the whole world. I am as you are, nameless, ageless, eternal. Together, in true humility, we stand in the Godhead."

He stood silent for a moment. Instantly his raiment was changed, he stood before us clothed as we were and at his side was a great Rajputana tiger. It was a beautiful beast, whose coat appeared like silken floss in the afterglow. A momentary fear swept over us, so engrossed had we been with the occurrence that we had been unconscious of the tiger's presence. Suddenly the animal crouched. A command from our guest and the tiger arose to its feet, walked forward and placed his muzzle in the man's outstretched hands. The wave of fear had swept over, leaving us calm. Our guest sat down before the campfire, while we drew close about him. The tiger walked a short distance away and stretched full length upon the ground.

Our guest said, "I have come to partake of your hospitality for a time and, if I am not intruding, I shall abide with you until the great mella." We all attempted to clasp his hand at once, so eager were we to extend a welcome.

He thanked us and began by saying: "You need not fear any animal. If you do not fear them, they will not harm you in any way.

"You have seen a body inactive on the ground before a village, for the protection of the inhabitants. That is only a physical sign to the people. The body is exposed, inactive, and at the mercy of the beast; though inactive, it remains unharmed and the people note that fact. Thus they lose all fear of the animal. The moment they have lost their fear, fear vibrations are not projected; and the animal, failing to pick up any fear vibrations, does not see the people as something to feed upon any more than he sees the tree, grass, or huts about him, as they project no vibrations of fear. The animal may pass directly through the same village where formerly he had selected the one he would feed upon, as that one was emanating the greatest fear. You have observed this. You have even observed the same animal stride directly over the prostrate form on the ground, walking directly through the village, looking for that which fears him.

"You observe the same animal walking directly between two small children less than twenty feet apart and attacking an older person that fears him. The children were not old enough to know fear; therefore, the animal did not see them."

Memories of these experiences came flooding back and we realized that we had not thought deeply enough upon the subject of fear to register its deeper meaning.

He then went on to say: "Love an animal and it must reciprocate with love; if it resists love, it will destroy itself before it can harm you. The animal is far more conscious of this condition than the human."

Glancing toward the tiger, he said: "Let us present love to our brother here and note the response."

We responded as best we could. Immediately the tiger rolled over, bounded to its feet and walked toward us, evidencing the greatest joy in every movement. The Rishi then resumed: "Approach the animal as your enemy and you have an enemy to contend with; approach him as a brother and you have a friend and protector."

The Muni who had accompanied us from the Tau Cross Temple, in Tibet, arose, announcing that he would leave us as he must return to Hardwar to serve the pilgrims that would be gathering for the mella. With an exchange of salutations, he left us. Although he had been very silent, we had enjoyed his comradeship beyond expression. There are many like him in this great land; they need not speak a word, yet you feel their greatness.

After the Muni had departed we sat down but had scarcely composed ourselves, when into the camp walked Emil, Jast, and Chander Sen. After an exchange of greetings we sat down and arranged an itinerary to tour a large portion of this country. When this was concluded, Emil related many of the interesting legends intimate with the places we would visit. Of these I shall record but one, as it relates to the district in which we were camped and had a most interesting and close association with the Maha Kumba mella that is held in this district every twelve years. To that mella and the shrines of this district there assemble more pilgrims annually than to any other district. Here assemble as many as five hundred thousand people at one mella. As this season's event would be of vast import, it was expected that this number would be augmented by hundreds of thousands. The auspiciousness of the event already pervaded the air.

Here food is provided for all pilgrims free during the mella. Hardwar is known as the Great Holy place. At Brindavan Sri Krishni lived and in this valley he grew to manhood. The district is a near-Paradise. This is the home of the sweet-songed bird, Kokila.

In this district stand the jewelled landmarks that came into existence where fell the drops of everlasting nectar as they were spilled from the jar of Amri, nectar which was cast up from the sea after the battle of Devatos (god) and Asura (demon) — in other words, of spirituality and gross materiality. This designates the time when India awakened to the vast import of spiritual life. This jar of nectar was so precious that a second battle was waged for its possession. Such was the haste of the god to out-distance the demon that drops were spilled from the jar; and where they fell these jewelled landmarks were erected.

This is a legend that veils the deeper spiritual meaning. That the meanings of these legends are permanent, everlasting, and far-reaching will be evidenced later.

Here in this district we wandered, visiting many temples, accompanying the Great Rishi. In December our Chief met us and we travelled south to Mount Abu. From there we returned to Brindavan and Hardwar and again visited many temples where we were accorded the most intimate and cordial associations with these people's lives. These intimate associations, teachings, and occasions cannot be published. The only restriction placed upon us was the request that, should we wish to give these out, we would do so personally to groups. In fact, the request was thaty they should not be written but should be given orally only to those who requested them.

The assembling of this great multitude of holy men and devotees is a never-to-be-forgotten experience. Here there is no hurry, confusion, or crowding among this vast throng, all travelling a direct route to one point for one purpose. One sees benevolence and kindness on every hand and hears the name of the most High, or the Almighty, on every lip, most reverently. It is a spiritual echo down the long, long corridor of what the western world calls Time. This has no import in the vastness of the East.

One can only imagine a great concourse of four or five hundred thousand people; there is no way of counting them.

As we were sitting before our campfire on the evening of the day preceding that of the great mella, the Rishi explained to us the purpose of this great event.

Nearly all these gatherings in India have a far deeper meaning than appears on the surface or than the repetition of the legend would imply.

CHAPTER XVII

T HE Rishi resumed: "But it is written, 'Eye hath not seen nor ear heard, neither hath entered into the heart of man the things which God hath prepared for them that love him.' [I Cor. 2:29.] This should have read, 'For them which love and bring forth the Christ of God.'

"Few understand Life's Principle or the purpose of Life. The Understanding Principle is that which stands under all things and is the principal thing. Therefore, it is a true proverb, 'With all thy getting, get understanding.' Understanding conscious purpose underlies everything. It was this that brought forth so proficiently for Solomon. He asked that the foundation of understanding be given to him and that an understanding heart be his. This opened to him such a fount of wisdom and led him to such a position of power, that there were bestowed upon him such riches and honor that he was known as the King of one thousand magnificent accomplishments. This has been symbolically spoken of as Solomon's 'thousand wives.'

"In Solomon's time, a wife was the symbol of a great accomplishment, an omniscient understanding which foresaw the whole history of the Universe and its definite connection with Humanity and each of its units. When Solomon gave out these accomplishments to his people and used them for their benefit, there were added to his store 'three thousand more' and his songs 'were a thousand and five.' 'And God gave Solomon wisdom and understanding exceeding much, and largeness of heart, even as the sand that is on the sea shore.' [I Kings 4:29-32.]

"Solomon was not a king in the literal or temporal sense of the word; he was a king over himself and his own household. This kingship he did hold. From that throne he dispensed love, understanding, wisdom, justice, and abundance to all that asked for wise counsel.

At that time all humanity was asking and, in response, he received love, understanding, wisdom, justice, and abundance a thousand fold. Although Solomon ruled them with a 'rod that standeth upright like iron,' it was the symbol of law that never fails. When that which he had sent out was magnified a thousand times ten thousand and returned with the same power, the Kingdom that Solomon held, though it were the whole earth, could not contain the richness of the reward of the law or lord that knew the treasure of the Christ of God, when he obeyed the command that the Self must come forth and obey God, Principle.

"Give with no thought of receiving and you cannot compass the reward. First give love to God, then to all the earth. When that love returns it has encompassed the whole earth and is magnified a thousand times ten thousand, as it has passed through the thoughts of millions of people and each has increased it one thousand times ten thousand fold. When it returns, is there room on earth for the fullness thereof?

"This alone has released earth and heaven is the result. Harmony reigns supreme. Solomon commanded of himself that he do this with understanding, wisdom, justice, abundance, and great joy. What happened? The earth could not hold the abundance; it was earth no more, it was Heaven.

"Do you wonder that those of Solomon's day called him a great King, a God? They fell down and worshipped Solomon, thinking that he could furnish them with every needed thing. This is where they erred; they did not realize that Solomon was the example that they should follow. God said unto Solomon: 'There shall be none like you in all the earth.' There could be none like him on earth for he had released the earthly estate; the heavenly estate was his and therein reigned his people as kingly as Solomon reigned. He set forth God, the heritage of man, which they must follow.

"Could such a King condemn one of his kings to death, when by doing so he condemned himself to the same death, multiplied one thousand times ten thousand? Such a king ruled justly, — not over other kings, but with kings, and there need be no pomp or glory of outer display. He need not even display his crown — all humanity knows of the crown. Such a King is a true ruler, not of the few, but with every human unit — they rule with him. This is man and God reigning supreme. This is the House of Israel, when the house becomes the tree, the root, the branch, the twig, the leaf, the flower, and the perfume that the flower emits, the very spirit of all races.

"Such a race did inhabit this earth and such a race will again inhabit this earth. I say unto you, you need not falter; heaven is here, if each human unit will but make it so.

"As men refuse to heed the call they will go out and return through birth into life, with its trials and tribulations; then through death again and again, until the lesson is finally learned — that upon the rock of absolute spiritual perception the whole human family is built.

"To such a race death does not exist nor can it again exist; therefore, Karma does not exist. Karma is but retribution for bringing into manifestation, discord, and inharmony. Substitute renunciation for retribution and you correct the cause for Karma, as it exists only in the thoughts of those determined to manifest Karma. Remove the cause or substitute it by a higher condition and the lower condition is erased. You have elevated the vibrations of your body above those which allowed Karma to exist.

"Death in no way removes Karma; neither does it destroy or erase it. Death adds to and magnifies Karma many fold, thus heaping it in great billows upon each human unit. The instant you let go of death and rebirth, you are free from death and Karma; both are erased. If erased, they are forgotten; if forgotten, they are forgiven.

"If at this stage, the absolute permanency of life cannot be perceived, thus conceived and brought into being, then there is an ultimate remedy for the mistake of death, named reincarnation.

"Reincarnation is but a guiding light on the blind trail of death. When this light leads, death may be overcome through round after round of earthly experiences. Then, through the lessons which those experiences teach, we arrive at the accomplishment of letting go of man-made conditions of creed or dogma that have been imposed upon us. Then we may again step forth into the full glory of God, into the light that is shining just as brightly, which has only seemed dim because we have wandered farther from the Father's House, the house of our own true self unalloyed by man-made creed and superstition.

"As we again approach the House, the light shines forth brighter with each advancing step; and, as we enter, we find it aglow with light and with the same warmth and beauty which only seemed dim through our outlook. There again we shall find quiet, peace, and rest; and in these we may feast at will. The same would have been ours had we entered the House before we wandered, creed and superstition-bound.

At the end of the trail all is forgotten and forgiven as it could have been before the beginning.

" 'Stand ye still and see the salvation of the Lord within you.' Stand completely still in the physical and see the complete salvation that the Lord Christ of God, standing forth as your true self, can give you. Thus, I perceived and stated the law that Abraham made use of so long ago. It is just as true this day as it was at that time. Manifestations take form as they are conceived in thought, word, or action, according to your belief. If the thought is not good, the remedy is, 'Change your thought. Call those things that be not, as though they were.'

"There are many mistakes in translation from the original texts to the context of your Bible, as well as many false prophecies. Many of these were brought about through lack of understanding of the characters and symbols with which the translators were dealing.

"These are excusable, as the translators were conscientious and their conclusions were presented as ably as they were able to comprehend them. The greater majority, however, were base falsehoods, perpetrated deliberately to mystify, to mislead, and to subvert the original gospel of the House of Israel.

"The first name was Is-rael, meaning the Crystal or pure white race, the first race that ever inhabited the world, the original or root race from which all other races sprang. This race was also designated as a pure light race, race, in many instances, meaning ray or beam. From this race sprang the Aryan race.

"The greater portion of this subversion of the Bible came about or began in the first and second centuries A.D. and this onslaught was directed in particular against the books of Daniel, Ezra, and Nehemiah. These misrepresentations were extended to the early works of Josephus and other books. They show conclusively that they were purposely perpetrated to hide well known data that existed at that time and instances that happened before that period. These falsifications were also instituted to destroy the definite chronological system and history preserved by the Israelites from the time consciousness began. Thousands of false histories of true events were written and substituted for originals and large portions of true historical data were distorted and effaced.

"The Aryan Race, a direct branch of this race, used this same chronological system and it has been preserved by them in its purity. Through this system, these forgeries and substitutions can be readily traced. Thus, we are in possession of true and complete Hebrew chronology. We know these falsehoods were extended to Solomon and to his household of wives, as well as to many others of the Ten Tribe House of Israel, its leaders, teachers, and counselors.

"After the division of this Ten Tribe House into two, the root kingdom was known as the House or Kingdom of Israel. The other was known as the tribe of Judah. While this tribe was of Israel, they were by no means all Israel. To hear Abraham, Isaac, and Jacob referred to as Jews is not only common error, but subversion; as only the descendants of Judah and those that came after, could be called after his name 'Jews.' The term 'Jew' was never applied to the Ten Tribe House of Israel nor to the twelve tribes of Israel.

"The Israelites were not Jews but the Jews were a tribe of the Israelitish Nation.

"When the tribe of Judah left Palestine and went into captivity, the name 'Jew' was applied to their tribe. Those that are known to us today as 'Jews' are the remnant of the tribe of Judah that returned to Palestine after they were released from captivity.

Many of them had mixed their blood with the surrounding nations. Those that call themselves 'Jews' today are less than one-third-blood of the real tribe of Judah.

"Wherever the Jews have lived and mingled with the Israelites or Aryans, they have flourished; and it is to these nations that they owe their hardihood. As time goes on, the Jews will see that it is to these nations that they will be obliged to turn for protection and succor and it behooves them to keep their house in order.

"That part of the tribe of Judah which joined the Israelites in their migrations through Europe are not a part of the race that are now known as the 'Jews.' That portion can in no way be distinguished from the other Israelites that settled in the British Isles and elsewhere and along the shores of the Mediterranean Sea, as through inter-marriage and environment they have all lost their tribal characteristics. I was of this race; therefore, I know.

"The Jews are with us; we can trace their history step by step, down the ages, from the House of Judah to the tribe of Judah, and down to the present day. They are one of the standing signs of the great race that has assisted in preserving the God ideal, until all races are restored into one race, with the Christ of God the controlling factor in each unit of that race, as it was before the great race began to disseminate and divide.

"It is not difficult to trace the migration of Israel from Jerusalem. The trails of those who settled in the British Isles are readily distinguishable. Likewise, that of the tribe of Dan. Their name and history, also the places where they settled, identify them. The Danube River, named from the tribe, is an open roadstead today, through which, after disseminating into tribes, divisions of these tribes came to Britain later as Danes, Jutes, Picts, and under other names as well. Thus, they went into Scandinavia, Ireland, Scotland, and other countries and, under these various names, they came to Britain and thence to America. As they reached America, they are in their former homeland. In this land of their origin, they are fast losing their tribal identities and are changing their language into the one language and that language will be the one which they spoke when they departed.

"They have wandered from home for a long, long time, but they are back again to their homeland; and that land extends to South America, Australia, New Zealand and the South Sea Islands and is as far flung as Japan and China.

"The Japanese and Chinese have migrated but little. They are divisions of a vital race that migrated from the motherland of Mu long before the disturbance that caused the mother continent to sink. They were called Uiguar or wandering tribes and are the progenitors of the Great Mongolian races. It is in this homeland that the white race achieved the highest civilization. They used emanating and radiating energy and released the energy of the atom to do useful work. They also developed levitation; thus they transported themselves from place to place. Their philosophy was entirely free from pagan worship, creed, dogma, and superstition. They worshipped true Principle as flowing through all humanity, man as divine as God.

"Israel-Arya is the symbol of the single and wise kingship and culture. From this race came the Bible and to this race its highest precepts were addressed.

"The Christ in man was their ideal. This was the torch that bore the light which was always aflame, the head of the sceptre. To fan this flame and keep it

160

glowing ever brighter, that man may never forget its precepts, those precepts were not only recorded in one Bible but in twelve Bibles.

"To guard against destruction or subversion, people built twelve corresponding Bibles in stone and located them throughout the Motherland. In order to bring them together under one head, thus making the precepts everlasting, they built the Great Pyramid; thus proving that the Christ, the foundation of civilization, was solidly established on earth among men and could not be defaced or erased. It would last forever, not only as a beacon that would hold high the light, but as a reflector for that light. It not only reflected the light but gave forth the oft-repeated command, 'If Humanity has lost the light, go within; there you will find recorded the precepts that will renew the light so that it may shine forth from you, the lost sheep that are wandering bereft of light.'

"With God, all that wander without the light (life) are sheep that have strayed from the fold. The fold is always there to behold and return to. The Christ, the shepherd, awaits with the lighted torch upheld for those that will enter therein. Although it has been hidden through the ages, it is always there for those that come, seeking the light.

"It is the first expression from the Cosmos. The voice, the word of God, comes forth. Here is LIGHT. LET THERE BE LIGHT, the vibration flashed forth; with those vibrations came LIFE. That Life is never separate from God, is witnessed by the fact that this Great Pyramid, with its foundation well established on earth, rears its head, uncrowned, to the skies.

"When man accepts his true heritage, Christ and the fact that the Christ of God is his true self in full

161

dominion, the crown or capstone will be placed; then will it stand as an everlasting witness to the fact that man will never again wander from the fold.

"The Great Pyramid is a Bible in stone, an indestructible bibliographical record portraying events of attainments and wanderings of God's chosen peoples. This does not mean just one people but *all people* who accept the Christ light. Neither does it give those people license to act and be less than Christ-like. It stands as a witness, lest humanity or its units wander away and forget, and dim this true Light, that from their midst would come forth One who had the determination fully to portray the Christ and with torch held high, aflame with light, would lead as the Christ within should lead.

"For ages, civilization has been going downward. In fact, so long has the great race trod the dark path, it appeared that this great race would lose its identity and revert to savagery and barbarism entirely. It was recognized that only a few were holding fast to the pure concepts that belonged to humanity, and that these few must withdraw into seclusion, in order that they could more readily come together, concentrate, and send out the light for the protection of humanity as a whole.

"Through this group, teachings were promulgated that the world needed a Savior, a God-man, who could and would step forth and, through thought, word, or deed teach and show humanity first through its units, then en masse, that the Christ still lived in them and was just as vital as ever, although inactive.

"The Christ light had been submerged by them because of their ignorance and refusal to live a Christ-like life. Through the spoken word, prophecy, and the heralding of groups and individuals, the proclamation was sent out to humanity that the Most

High had appointed a Savior, who would again live true to humanity's highest concepts, and that a Savior would come forth at an appointed time.

"This was an edict of the Most High which the Godhead poured out through a group of human units. Those units saw that, in order to attract men to the Savior who would come among them, it would be necessary to set an appointed time for His advent and that all should be instructed as to the method and purpose of His coming, even fixing the exact date of the crucifixion.

"This was not only necessary in order to give His teachings greater weight and vitality, but it was necessary to bring humanity's thoughts back to a focal or central point, as the majority were wandering entirely after strange gods. Humanity had gone so far afield that spiritual death was imminent. Thus, it was proclaimed that the body of this Messiah or Savior would be slain and that his body would be placed in a rock-hewn tomb and a complete resurrection would follow. Thus, humanity would again be shown that they could turn from being the 'sons of men' and become the Sons of God, — the Christ of God always dwelling One with God. Thus, by living the God life, man would never go back into the welter; peace and good will would reign on earth. It was also written that this condition did exist and was before all things and that He would teach them man's true heritage. Thus He did exist and was the Hidden One of the ages; and through the precepts that He taught, flowed the fountain of God's providence and the full fruits of the earth that were for man's free use.

"These prophecies had become paganized and subverted before the advent of Jesus; and this subversion has extended to this day, leading many to believe that the basic elements of Christianity had been borrowed from previous religions, instead of knowing that it has always stood forth and accomplished humanity's highest ideal.

"The body of the mother, the one who would bring forth and nourish this Christ Child, and the body of the father who would stand as a physical protector, were also prepared for this immaculate birth, each complete yet united as one, to watch over this child who would grow into maturity among those he would teach.

"The mother was Mary and the father was Joseph, both representing the descendants of David, the true light-bearer; from the seed of Abraham, meaning Ah Brahm, the bearer of the complete light from the great Cosmos.

"The sons of man had reverted so low in the scale that the vibrations of their bodies were below those of the animal. By stepping forth and presenting the long-forgotten Christ, He knew full well they would attempt to ravage his body in a greater degree than the animal would. Unless human perceptions are guided by the Christ light, they will sink lower than the animal.

"He knew He must be so definitely at-one with the Christ in His dominion that they could not touch Him unless He chose. Thus, He was fearless in choosing the rôle. Such an One choosing this rôle must be humble, knowing fully that such is the rôle that all have followed through their Christ life.

"This gathering consolidates this idea more definitely. You can observe the silent influence wielded through the thousands of humble souls gathered here. You can calculate this fully by taking for the basis of your deductions the fact that one man, standing forth in his Godhead, giving forth in fullest measure, conquers the world and death is no more. Add to this the influence of one more who is as powerful, the influence of the two is four-fold greater than the one. Then multiply this by the numbers gathered here and you can realize the power that is radiating forth to the whole world from this multitude.

"With such a power center in full radiation, the world is reborn, revitalized, and renewed instantly, whether the units of humanity realize it or not. Such an assembly has gathered in stated locations throughout the world every twelve years, far down the ages, long before Neptune threw off her mantle of God. Their numbers were less in the earlier days, but the radiations going out from the groups have attracted others without an audible word being spoken.

"The first small group grew into a multitude; then one from that multitude formed another group, and so on, until twelve groups were formed; and this is the twelfth or last group, making thirteen in all. This group has assembled to consolidate and unite the twelve with the first group, making thirteen united into one complete group, yet meeting as the original groups have met, in different places, to facilitate the accessibility of the assembling places.

"There is no attempt at definite organization; neither are there any hard and fast rules adhered to. It is only organized as each individual is organized within and, through that organization, is drawn to one of the groups. The location of the assemblies has never been revealed to people in general, which proves that there has been no attempt at organization.

"The assembly which will gather at twelve o'clock tomorrow will fully consolidate all the groups under the first group, the twelve building a pyramid symbolizing the completion of the Christ ideal in man, the thirteenth constituting the capstone or crown.

"All the thirteen groups will assemble as separate groups in the same location as before; yet the assembling of one or all of the groups will be the same as though all were meeting with the head group, which will be accomplished tomorrow.

"Aside from just assembling for consolidation of the thirteen groups into one group, twelve from each of the twelve groups will go out to assist in forming twelve more groups. Multiply this by twelve, which will be one hundred and forty-four groups. When these groups are augmented by other units of humanity, they will again branch out into groups of twelve. Thus a pyramid formed of groups in the order of twelve will be erected until it encompasses the earth.

"The only requisite necessary to become one or a part of these groups is first to present the Christ ideal to yourself, then give forth Christ to the world in thought, word and deed. You are then one with this whole great group and where you meet God, they must meet with you, in your home, your own sanctuary, be it in the most remote part of the world, on the mountain peak, or in the busy marts of trade. *One with God* is the determining factor always. The instant you lift your thought to the Christ, your body responds to the Christ vibration; then you respond to the same vibratory influence that is emanating from this vast throng and the multiplied energy of its numbers picks up your Christ ideal and spreads it broadcast to the whole world; and your influence is carried on and on with the combined whole in a great tidal wave of thought.

"Thus, instead of remaining in the former seclusion, these precepts will become world-wide. To such a group there need be no head, save the Great Godhead of the whole human race; no form, no sect, no creed is necessary.

"Declare you are the Christ and command the self to live true to this ideal concept in thought, word and deed; thus you do conceive and bring forth the Christ. These vibrations once established are never diminished, though the unit or individual be unconscious of their existence; but if you keep on and on, you will become conscious of these vibrations— which is a far greater experience than any other could be. Thus, the focal point which is established is true and can never be erased; and to this point every human unit must eventually come. To such the whole wide vista of the Universe is opened and there are no restrictions added to or imposed upon the individual. The vista imposed by the human vision may be outside these vibrations, but it may be brought within the range of vibratory vision. There may not appear to be an individual here within the vibratory ray which the human vision imposes, but each is here and we recognize him. You, who have walked or ridden all the way, have at times glimpsed this fact or you would not be here.

"With such a united humanity, can the battle of Gog and Magog or Armageddon be fought? Can man-made manifestations of law bring forth a force that will trample over God Law, which is ruling above and co-existing with all force? Here but one God-man need say, 'NO,' and it will be accomplished, as all are in unison and respond in unison. No force need be exerted. The force to harm that those in the lower vibrations are sending out can be concentrated and returned to them with true love and blessing. If they resist, they will but destroy themselves; and those who are returning the love force need not so much as lift a hand.

"These groups stand as the Great Pyramid has stood, indestructible down through the ages, as a witness, in stone, to humanity that the Christ in man was fully established long before man's advent, and that man as the Christ has never been separated from the Godhead. That this Great Pyramid is such a witness is fully established by its age and purity of form, construction, and intellectual value. It has been preserved and mentioned as the Great Pyramid throughout millennia. All the scientific information that is imbedded in the huge mass was not placed there for the advancement of science, as men must be well versed in science in order to interpret its knowledge.

"Its great antiquity and wonderful structure have set it aside as a mystery to mankind. Within its mass is exposed the secret of the Universe; each delineation is in precise terms and methods of exact science. This was pre-ordained and is working toward the harmonious consummation of man standing forth as the Christ of God, completely amalgamated with God. The culmination of this accomplishment will place the capstone upon the Great Pyramid."

CHAPTER XVIII

A S THE RISHI finished, a number of people walked toward our camp and Jesus was in the group. We had noted that they had gathered on the slope of the ridge a short distance from the camp but had supposed that they were gathering for a private conference, as these gatherings were in evidence all about the countryside.

As they approached, Weldon arose, stepped forward, and clasped both of Jesus' hands. There was no need for an introduction, as they were all close friends of the Rishi and Jesus. As for ourselves, we felt like little atoms ready to take root in any niche where soil presented itself.

All gathered around our campfire. Weldon asked Jesus if he would talk to us of the Bible. This met with a most hearty approval from all and Jesus began:

"Let us consider David's prayer in the twenty-third psalm, 'The Lord is my shepherd, I shall not want.' You will note this was not a prayer of supplication. Do you not see that the real meaning implies that the One great Principle is leading us into the way we should go, or Great Principle goes before on our pathway, and thus we make the crooked places straight? This Principle prepares our pathway as a shepherd does for his trusting and dependent sheep; thus we can say, 'Where Our Father leads I am unafraid.'

"The good shepherd knows where everything is located that is good for his sheep; thus we can say, 'I shall not want.' With David we can say, 'I cannot want,' for I AM is guarded against every ill.

"Every want of our physical nature is supplied. Not only shall we be well fed in the green pastures but there will be an abundance to spare. We rest in complete assurance that every desire is already fulfilled and provided for. We can let go of every weary sense and say, with David, 'He maketh me to lie down in green pastures, He leadeth me beside still waters.' The blue of their quiet depths gives great peace to our minds and our troubled consciousness is stilled.

"With body and mind at rest, the heavenly inspiration of the most high Principle floods our souls with the pure light of life and power. The light within us glows with the glory of my Lord, the law wherein we are all one. This radiant light of spirit renews our understanding; we stand revealed to our true selves, so that we know ourselves as one with the Infinite and each is sent from this Principle to manifest the perfection of the Father Principle. In the quiet calm of our souls, we are restored to our pure selves and know that we are whole; thus, 'He restoreth my soul. Yea though I walk through the valley of the shadow of death, I will fear no evil.' In the fullness of the bounty of this God Principle, what can we fear? Here we rest our physical natures, God quiets our minds, God rests our souls, God illumines us for service; therefore, with this perfect preparation from within, what outer tests could cause us to fear that any evil thing could harm us? God is in the midst of every one of us; to each he is an ever-present help in time of trouble. In Him we live and move and have our being. We say with one voice, 'All is well.'

"Now each can say, 'God love leads me directly into the fold. I am shown the right path and corrected when I stray from this fold. The power of God love attracts me to my good; thus all that would harm is shut from me.'

"Now, with David, each can say, 'For thou art with me, thy rod and thy staff they comfort me.'

"In first taking up this work and perceiving the truths or the fundamental scientific facts underlying all life and the way of attaining thereto, you take the first step, and the exhilaration and enlightenment are so far beyond anything you have hitherto experienced that you decide to go on in the work. Then doubts, fears, and discouragements are allowed to creep in and your on-going seems to be retarded. You struggle first one way, then another, and you seem to be losing ground. The struggle seems to be too great for human beings to accomplish and you begin to look at the failures all about you.

"You say God's children are dying on every hand and none within your generation has accomplished the ideal of everlasting and eternal life, peace, harmony, and perfection which I idealize. You say that accomplishment must come after death; so you let go and find for a time that it is much easier to drift on and on with the human tide on the downward trend.

"Again, the race consciousness has had another setback; another who had a great spiritual enlightenment and understanding and could have succeeded, has failed and the race consciousness has another binding hold upon humanity. Generation after generation gives it a still greater and tenacious grip. Is it any wonder that human nature becomes weak and frail; and each in turn follows on and on, in the same eternal treadmill, the blind following the blind, on and on into eternal oblivion; and into the great vortex, where not only the body is forced into dissolution and decay, but the soul is ground between the never-relenting millstones of human perception and mistakes?

"If you would realize, as I did and as so many have

171

done, that it is far easier to work out your own problem in one earthly experience than it is to go on and on and accumulate a race consciousness of good and evil that soon becomes an encrusted shell; that has been added to, layer by layer, upon an encrustation by each succeeding experience, until it takes superhuman force and sledge-hammer blows to break the shell and release your true self.

"Until you do break the shell and release your true self, you will continue to be ground in the same vortex. You can work until you have released yourself sufficiently to get a glimpse of the horizon's 'grander view.' Here again you cease to struggle, your mental vision is cleared, but your body is still encased in the shell. Realize that the newborn chick, when its head is free from its shell, must still go on with the struggle. It must be entirely free from its old shell or environment before it can grow into the new, which it has sensed and perceived as soon as it has broken a hole through the shell once encasing the egg from which it grew.

"You fail utterly to see that I, as a boy working at the carpenter's bench with my father, perceived that there was a higher life for the God-born so-called human being than to be born into a human existence for a short time and, during that short existence, be ground between the millstones of man-made laws, superstitions, and conventions and thus struggle on through that existence for perhaps three score years and ten, then pass on to a heaven and a glorious reward of harps and psalm singing that could have no logical existence except in the gullible minds of those preyed upon by the priesthood of my day.

"You fail utterly to see that, after this great awakening or realization within myself, it took long days and nights of struggle in seclusion and silence, all alone, right within myself and with myself. Then, when the self was conquered, it took the far greater and more bitter experiences of personal contact with those I loved dearly and to whom I wished to show the light that I had perceived; knowing it was the light that burns so brightly, lighting the path of every child of God that is created or that comes into the world.

"You fail utterly to see the great temptation that beset me to go on and be the carpenter I might have been and thence live the short span of life allotted to man by hierarchy and orthodoxy; instead of taking up a life which perception had only given me a glimpse of, thus allowing me to see through the murk and mire of superstition, discord, and disbelief.

"You fail utterly to follow the bodily anguish, the ignominious insults that were heaped upon me by my own kin alone, aside from those to whom I strove to show the light I had perceived. You failed to see that this took a will stronger than my own, which sustained me through these trials. How little you can know of the trials and struggles, temptations, and defeats that beset me. How, at times, I struggled on and on with clenched fists and set teeth, seeing and knowing that the light was there; although there seemed to be but one last flickering ray and, at times, it seemed that that last ray had gone out and a shadow was cast in its place. Even then, something within me was ever strong and dominant, that, back of the shadow, the light was as bright as ever. I went on and cast aside the shadow and found the light burning even brighter because of the temporary dimming. Even when the shadow proved to be the cross and I could see beyond; the final awakening of a triumphant morn that passed beyond the understanding of mortal man, still immersed in fear, doubts, and superstitions. It was the very urge of this perception that sent me on, determined to drink the cup to the fullest draft, that I might know by actual experience and contact whereof I spoke; that man by the free will of God, coupled with his own free thought and pure motive, could prove for himself alone that God is divine; and that man, His true son, born in His image and likeness, is as truly divine as the Father is divine; and that this divinity is the true Christ that every man sees and perceives, is in himself and in all of God's children.

"This true Christ is the light that lights every child that comes into the world. It is the Christ of God our Father, in, through, and by whom we all have everlasting life, light, love, and true brotherhood — the true Fatherhood, the true Sonship, of God and man.

"In the light of this true understanding or Truth, you do not need a king, a queen, a crown, a pope or a priest. You, in the true perception, are the king, the queen, the pope, the priest; and none but yourself and God stand alone. You expand this true perception to take in the whole Universe of form and shape; and with your God-given creative ability, you surround them with the perfection that God sees and surrounds them with."

ADDENDUM

The word *Arya* means cultured, refined, noble.
Aryavarta was the land wherein the people gave
great heed to race culture.
Arya-bhava was the ancient name for the highest
virtue.
Arya-marga was the path to noble life.
These precepts had been handed down through
eons of time.

In ancient India, culture was most human in its
outlook, the thought being "great men for a great
country"; hence we find a great people, complete
brotherhood, true love and reverence for each human unit, truly humble souls knowing that all are
God. This could in no way become another name for
strife and contention; it must become the dominant
factor in its essential relationship toward the building of true world consciousness.

The Aryans dreamed and philosophized; yet their
dreams were most real. They not only dreamed of
God, they knew that God was actually enthroned in
the hearts and lives of all mankind, as the true and
beautiful in every human unit.

Is there an intelligent man that does not have such
a philosophy, a viewpoint or attitude toward the
world? What better attitude could there be than
viewing the world through the eyes of the God-man?
Is it not through this attitude that all humanity lives
richer and more harmonious lives?

The Aryan message is, "Build up your manhood
and womanhood and you build up all humanity." By
so doing, you avoid the so-called sins against the
body. Through the accomplishment of this ideal,

you realize the supreme opportunity of earth's pilgrimage and, with the right sense of proportion, the rich powers of youth are laid as an offering at the Mother's Shrine. Thus, you find the key to the kingdom of heaven right within your own soul, just as you did a thousand or a million years back and will do in the years to come.

This can be accomplished here and now; or you can go on and plow through materiality on its network of roads and through its network of thoughts, until you eventually reach the same central white light which is again Spirit, the Christ in every one, the truth made manifest unto you. This is the ultimate for all races, all creeds, all religions, the Fatherhood and Motherhood of God.

Once self-mastery is attained, the Master leads on and on, ever on.

The Aryan manhood guarded Aryan culture. The Aryan womanhood has been the greatest guardian of this culture. All through the ages, she has nourished the moral, social, and political life; her intuitions and mysticism of sympathy have always stood as the great bulwark of the Aryan Ideal.

Aristotle asked that an Indian teacher, versed in the ancient teachings and culture of India, be brought to him — a teacher that in the noblest sense could be called a true man, physically strong, intellectually and morally refined.

It is God's promise that prayer is always answered. "I say unto you, ask and it is given unto you, seek and ye shall find, knock and it is opened unto you. For every one that asketh, receiveth; and he that seeketh findeth; and to him that knocketh, it shall be opened."

In other words, the Christ admonishes us, "When Principle says, 'Yes,' refuse to take, 'No.'" *No* does not have its origin in God but in our own failure to believe in God's promise. The God-promise to man never fails, but how few can stand the test of knowing. How few can meet every trial by knowing God, until the Christ of God is released within them.

What an invitation to constantly know God; what an appeal for definiteness and persistency.

God Principle always bears with its own, those ready to receive the highest understanding. As they cry out for deliverance from their adversaries, they know it is only for their future purification and enlightenment. Thus, they realize that the adversary is a friend, as the adversary compels their unceasing search for God Principle.

The promise is, "Principle cannot break its own law." We ask for strength to erase the evil thought that law can be broken or that there is a power that can oppose God Power. As God is all Power, God must answer prayer.

GOD IS THE ONLY WORD, IT CANNOT FAIL.

—B. T. S.

For a Complete Price List of
Inspirational, Self-help & Metaphysical Books,
write to:

DeVorss & Co., *Publishers*
P.O. Box 550
Marina del Rey, CA 90294